THE QUEEN
& HER COURT

THE QUEEN & HER COURT

A GUIDE TO
THE BRITISH MONARCHY
TODAY

JERROLD M. PACKARD

CHARLES SCRIBNER'S SONS
NEW YORK

Copyright © 1981 Jerrold M. Packard

Library of Congress Cataloging in Publication Data

Packard, Jerrold M.
The Queen & her court.

  Bibliography: p.
  Includes index.
  1. Elizabeth II, Queen of Great Britain,
1926–   2. Monarchy, British.   3. Windsor,
House of.   4. Great Britain—Court and courtiers.
I. Title.
DA590.P25   941.085′092′2   80-29232
ISBN 0-684-17648-3

1 3 5 7 9 11 13 15 17 19   F/P   20 18 16 14 12 10 8 6 4 2

Printed in the United States of America

The Royal Arms on page 191 are reproduced by permission from
The British Monarchy in Colour by John Brooke-Little,
published by Blandford Press, Poole, Dorset, England.

For Merl

Contents

Introduction

"I've been waiting for this for thirty years."
—Mrs. Eva Hoe, *as she sat on a fence, having
traveled 25 miles from her home to watch the
Queen pass through Hull.*

If measured in terms of its sheer power to mesmerize tens of millions of people both at home and abroad, the British monarchy is the most fascinating institution on earth. Where its ordinary human activities can capture every newspaper headline in the Western world, its great cataclysms—love affairs, deaths, crownings, scandals—invoke a kind of manic media glare that is astonishing in its intensity. The lives of the chief members of the royal family have been chronicled to the point of absurdity: by the age of 30, Prince Charles had been the subject of at least a dozen biographies, some serious, some fluff. Their foibles have been blown out of all proportion: Charles's unguarded comment concerning his cousin's marriage to a Roman Catholic created a religious storm felt from the Vatican to Lambeth Palace. The places where they live are icons for their idolizers as well as for the merely curious; Buckingham Palace acts as a giant magnet to the hundreds of tourists peering through its gates from dawn to midnight.

But in spite of the massive publicity which constantly envelops the throne and nearly everything remotely connected with it, the monarchy remains a tangle of half-com-

1

prehended mysteries. This book is intended as a sort of road map through the thicket of detail surrounding the Crown—if you will, a *vade mecum* to Britain's monarchy.

It may seem surprising that the anachronism that is Britain's Crown and Court can survive—and with general approbation—in a world no longer much beholden to the quixotical. It is hoped that this book will contribute to a better understanding of the monarchy and to what the monarchy means not only to Great Britain but to the world.

1

Family
THE WINDSOR MATRIARCHY

Elizabeth the Second, by the Grace of God of the United Kingdom of Great Britain and Northern Ireland and Her other Realms and Territories Queen, Head of the Commonwealth, Defender of the Faith. Such is the official title of the British monarch. But it is the far plainer title of "Queen of England" by which she is known. Not Queen of Great Britain, nor of the United Kingdom, but simply "of England." This unadorned title geographically encompasses only a part of the island of Britain itself, omitting Scotland and Wales, yet it is the proudest title of royalty in history. Beside it, all the emperors and overlords and grand sachems—now mostly long gone—have second or lesser place.

Queen Elizabeth II can trace her descent from King Egbert, who in A.D. 829 united England under his crown. In the next eleven and a half centuries, the continuity of that crown would be broken only once—for the eleven years from 1649 to 1660, under the Cromwellian republic. No existing secular institution on earth predates the English monarchy. The Crown anticipated the English Parliament by four centuries, the English law courts by three.

The inflexible law of the monarchy has been the principle of hereditary succession. Although there were deviations from this precept before the reign of King George I, the principle itself has been preserved. The rules of hereditary succession will be fully explained in a later chapter, but briefly, they provide that the Crown goes from fathers to sons and their sons in order of seniority, or in the absence of sons to daughters in order of seniority; in the event the sovereign leaves no descendants, it passes to his eldest surviving brother, and so on. There is a logical and ironclad order of succession, and the individuals within that order can be charted to a seemingly endless number.

There are three ways of defining what constitutes Britain's "royal family." The smallest unit today is the Queen, her husband, her three sons, and her daughter and son-in-law. Usually this group is extended to include the Queen Mother and Princess Margaret and her son and daughter. The broadest definition takes in the families of the Queen's father's two younger brothers. Rarely is the family of the Queen's only paternal aunt, the late Princess Royal (Princess Mary), included in today's reckoning of the royal family.

The easiest way to clarify these relationships is to trace the family members from the Queen's paternal grandfather, King George V. George himself wasn't born in *direct* line of succession to the throne. (Direct line normally includes only the eldest son, his eldest son, and so on.) His father's mother was Queen Victoria, who was to reign for 36 years after George's birth in 1865. George was the son of the Prince of Wales, Victoria's oldest son and heir who became King Edward VII on his mother's death in 1901.

George was only the second son. His elder brother, Prince Albert Victor, was in direct line of succession. Albert Victor was, at the very least, dim-witted and quite possibly mildly retarded. With his growth into young manhood, he became an embarrassment to the royal family, and a great deal of anxiety was caused by his benumbed lack of maturity and intelligence. (Apparently no thought was given to removing him from the line of succession, something which certainly had no constitutional precedent; besides, the general public didn't know there was anything wrong with Eddy, and if it had, the knowledge would have been extremely detrimental to the Crown.) His grandmother created him Duke of Clarence and Avondale, and in time he became engaged to his cousin, Princess May of Teck. Before the marriage could take place, Prince Eddy, as his family called him, died of the combined effects of syphilis and pneumonia, an event which then put George in the direct line of succession, with only his father standing between himself and the throne. Princess May had in the meantime shown herself to be such a desirable future Queen of England while betrothed to Eddy that her engagement was simply transferred to George 18 months after Eddy's death. Thus Princess May eventually became Queen Mary, consort to King George V.

An interesting sidelight emerges in the case of Prince Eddy. A number of researchers have concluded that the young man who, had he lived, would have become King of England was the murderer known to history as Jack the Ripper. No incontrovertible evidence has linked Prince Eddy with the slayings of several London prostitutes, but a recently published book concludes that Eddy was indeed the killer, based on strong circumstantial evidence. While the truth may never be known, it is a safe conclusion that England's monarchial system was done a great favor by Eddy's early demise.

So Prince George ("Georgy"), who had been made Duke of York while his father was still Prince of Wales, himself was given the title of Prince of Wales when his parents ascended the throne as King Edward VII and Queen Alexandra in 1901. George was a conservative's conservative, an absolute model of benign reaction. Since his views didn't much affect politics, his reaction found its principal influence in George's private and semiprivate lives. But his arch-Victorian upper-class rectitude gained the favor of a British public antagonistic to his father's wild ways. King Edward VII was a voluptuary pure and simple. His life was lived for pleasure, and anything that came between him and his fleshly amusements wasn't likely to detain him for long.

When after a short reign Edward died in 1910, his son came to the throne as George V. The most exemplary period of George's reign was during World War I. He and Queen Mary served as the perfect symbols of British virtue. They became beloved by their people, but from a distance much further than that to which today's royal family is accustomed. In the time of George V, the royal family was held in a demigodlike thrall, and the public knew relatively little of the more human and domestic aspects of their lives.

George and Mary had six children. The oldest was Edward, called David by his family. He became Prince of Wales and later King Edward VIII; when lastly he became Duke of Windsor, the throne underwent its most severe jolting in modern times. The second son was Albert, nicknamed Bertie. When he came of age he was given the title of Duke of York, available since it had been vacated by his father on becoming Prince of Wales. Bertie later became King George VI when his elder brother abdicated. Next was Mary, the only girl; by her marriage into the nobility she would become the Countess of Harewood, and was later declared Princess Royal. The third son was Henry, called Harry, and named Duke of Gloucester on his coming of age. George, who would be titled Duke of Kent, was next, and the most handsome of the brood. Last was Prince John, almost completely unknown to the public, and who died of epilepsy at the age of 13 in 1919. This youngest son lived apart from the family in his own house, Wood Farm on the Sandringham estate, apparently being forced to do so because it was believed that his condition was either shameful or contagious.

King George V celebrated his Silver Jubilee in 1935, marking 25 years as King. At the same time, England's greatest modern royal crisis was beginning to brew in earnest. The heir to the throne, the Prince of Wales, had fallen in love with someone manifestly unsuitable to be Queen of England. Wallis Warfield Spencer Simpson was a divorced woman still married to her second husband. Soon after the king died in January 1936, David, as the new King Edward VIII, decided he couldn't do without Mrs. Simpson, and wouldn't merely keep her by his side in the role of a mistress. As king, Edward was also constitutionally "defender of the faith," that is, the Church of England—an institution which couldn't countenance divorce for the king's wife for any reason. The story is familiar beyond need to detail; Edward abdicated in December 1936 and became the new Duke of Windsor, a title his brother Albert, who became the new King George VI, granted him the following spring (he was known simply as "Prince Edward" in the interim). England was undoubtedly well rid of Edward VIII. Never displaying the same sense of constitutional monarchy that his father did in his reign and his brother would in his, David wasn't able to separate the person of the King from the significance of the office. Even his seemingly petty actions were telling in retrospect: he broke a 300-year-old custom that sovereigns alternate their profiles on the country's coinage, currency and stamps—left profile one reign, right the next, and so on. He demanded his right profile be shown, considering it his "best side." He had his way, but his brother Bertie also used *his* right profile in his reign, continuing the tradition just as if his elder brother had followed the correct custom.

Albert, who had been christened Albert Frederick Arthur George, chose to be known as George during his reign so as to stress continuity with King George V's stability and to disassociate himself from his brother's disastrous 11-month reign. He had been married in 1923 to the daughter of the Earl and Countess of Strathmore, Lady Elizabeth Bowes-Lyon, and thus became the first sovereign married to a commoner since James II married Anne Hyde (as will be fully explained in Chapter V). When still Duke and Duchess of York, they had two daughters, Elizabeth, born in 1926, and Margaret Rose, born in 1930.

On her father's accession in 1936, Princess Elizabeth became Heiress Presumptive to the throne. Had she been a boy, she would have been Heir Apparent, and undoubtedly would have soon been named Prince of Wales, the title of the direct male heir to England's crown. But it had to be "presumed" that she could have been dislodged from first place in succession to the crown by the birth of a brother. As it was, even had they wished to have more children after coming to the throne, it simply wasn't possible for the busy new queen to spare the months necessary for a confinement, then a much more socially delicate matter than today. Besides, King George liked his neat and cozy family just as it was and didn't want to change it, especially since another daughter might be the only result. The young Princess Elizabeth hence began being groomed by her father as the future sovereign.

In this change from Duke and Duchess of York to King and Queen, their younger daughter went, in her own words, from being "Princess Margaret of York to Princess Margaret of Nothing." Her grievance had merit, since children of the sovereign have no "territorial" title beyond Prince or Princess (even the eldest son's title of Prince of Wales is not automatic, being conferred only when the sovereign wishes to do so). Not too much sympathy should be tendered however, as the loss of part of a title represented a considerable advance in rank.

Meanwhile, others of King George V's children were marrying and starting families. First had been Princess

Mary, who in 1922 took as her husband a man 15 years her senior, the son and heir of the fifth Earl of Harewood, who then bore the courtesy title of Viscount Lascelles. Mary's new title became "HRH Princess Mary, the Viscountess Lascelles." Her husband inherited the earldom in 1929, changing the last part of the princess's title to Countess of Harewood. Two years later there was another name change when her father made her Princess Royal; it was as such that she died in 1965. The couple, whose marriage soon turned to indifference, had two sons, George and Gerald. George, who became a musical administrator and director of the English National Opera, inherited the earldom on his father's death in 1947.

Like his parents' marriage, George's too turned sour. Unlike his parents', his ended in divorce, with his wife suing him for adultery in 1967. He immediately remarried, to an Australian, Patricia "Bambi" Tuckwell, his former secretary who had borne him a son, Mark, in 1964. The son born in 1950 by his first marriage to Marion Stein (today the wife of Jeremy Thorpe, the Liberal Party leader tried and acquitted in 1980 for conspiring the murder of his alleged homosexual lover) is the heir to the earldom and the present Viscount Lascelles. This potentially scandalous divorce had minimal effect on the Crown. The Queen assented to Harewood's remarriage, which the Royal Marriages Act of 1772 requires to make the union legal in Britain, with very little fuss. The new Countess of Harewood is not, however, considered even a peripheral member of the royal family, a fact brought home when the Harewoods were pointedly not invited to Princess Anne's wedding.

The second Harewood son, Gerald Lascelles, also had his first marriage dissolved. In 1978, he divorced his wife of 26 years, Angela Dowding, by whom he had one son, Henry Ulick. He married Mrs. Elizabeth Colvin later the same year.

The next child of George V was the Queen's last surviving paternal uncle, Henry, Duke of Gloucester. (Her
oldest royal uncle, the Duke of Windsor, died in 1972, forever embittered with his family because his wife was not
granted the style of "Royal Highness" as were the wives of
his other brothers. At least the present Queen has given permission for her to be buried on royal ground beside her husband when she dies.) Of the brothers, Henry was the
homeliest as an adult, and the dullest, with the least natural
panache. Even his wedding was relatively routine, to the
plain Alice Montagu-Douglas-Scott, a daughter of the enor-
mously rich Duke of Buccleuch and Queensberry, and a direct descendant of King Charles II through his illegitimate
son by Lucy Walter, the unfortunate Duke of Monmouth (a
swaggering fool who had his head cut off for treason against
his father). The Duke of Buccleuch (pronounced Ba-cloo)
died just before his daughter's marriage, which caused the
cancellation of a State wedding at Westminster Abbey and
the substitution of a small private ceremony at Buckingham
Palace, putting another touch of glum on Harry. The
Gloucesters had two sons, William and Richard. The oldest,
William, was killed in 1972 at the age of 30 when he crashed
his Piper Cherokee at the start of the Goodyear Air Race.
This left the younger son to succeed to the dukedom on his
father's death in 1974.

Richard, nicknamed "Proggie" (from the acronym
PRG—Prince Richard of Gloucester) at Cambridge, is a
quiet, good-looking young man who resembles nobody in his
family. The 36-year-old prince is a graduate of Cambridge in
architecture, a real accomplishment in the royal family. He
has had to shelve any thoughts of a career so that he can
carry out royal engagements on behalf of his cousin the
Queen. His wife, the new Duchess of Gloucester, was Birgitte van Deurs, the daughter of a Danish lawyer. Their
1972 wedding was not a traditional royal London affair, but

took place instead near Barnwell Manor, the 40-room Gloucester mansion on 2,500 acres of working farmland 80 miles north of the capital. Their children are Alexander, Earl of Ulster (the Duke's second title), born in 1974, Lady Davina Windsor, born in 1977, and Lady Rose Windsor, born in 1980.

Princess Alice, Dowager Duchess of Gloucester, is still an active working member of the royal family, and serves as an honorary Air Marshal of the Women's Royal Air Force, as well as a number of regimental colonelcies. She carries out several dozen formal engagements each year, and by way of a pastime is a fairly accomplished watercolorist.

The youngest of the four sons of George V who survived into manhood was George, Duke of Kent. He was an unusually attractive man, and, unfortunately, a narcotics addict in the early thirties, the result of a flirtation with drugs caused by a depression over an unhappy love affair. He suffered a nervous breakdown while trying unsuccessfully to break the habit, but with his brother David's help, he was eventually able to overcome his addiction. In 1934, he married the beautiful Princess Marina of Greece, a granddaughter of Greece's King George I. Marina was considered one of the prize catches of the decade. Together, the Duke and Duchess made a dashing couple, and after their State wedding in Westminster Abbey were very popular in Britain, epitomizing that era's royal chic.

George and Marina had three children: Edward, Alexandra and Michael. The Duke was killed while on active Air Force service in 1942, and was succeeded by his son Edward (called Eddie by family and friends) as the second Duke of Kent. After graduating from Sandhurst (Britain's West Point) in 1953, the young duke was commissioned in the Royal Scots Dragoon Guards and served in Germany, Hong Kong, Cyprus and Northern Ireland, rising on his own merits to the rank of lieutenant colonel. In 1975, he retired from the army after 23 years of service, and became Vice-Chairman of the British Overseas Trade Board (an organization which markets British technology overseas), which he had joined the previous year.

The Duke married Katharine Worsley in 1961, a strikingly beautiful blonde English countrywoman and daughter of a baronet, as well as the only descendant of Oliver Cromwell to have so far married into the royal family. The Kent children are George, Earl of St. Andrews, born in 1962, Lady Helen Windsor, born in 1964, and Lord Nicholas Windsor, born in 1970.

Alexandra married the second and therefore titleless son of the Earl of Airlie, the Honorable Angus Ogilvy, a London businessman and member of numerous corporate boards. In her mid-40s, Princess Alexandra is a beautiful and popular woman, carrying out many royal functions for the Queen. Most Britons consider her the best of the "junior" members of the royal family, but Ogilvy was thought by many to be rather boorish for refusing a proferred earldom when he married Alexandra. His business dealings came in for a good deal of criticism in the recent scandal involving the British mining company, Lonrho, of which he was a director. Their children are James, born in 1964, and Marina, born in 1966.

The youngest Kent son, Michael, born only a month before his father's death in 1942, carries out no independent official royal duties. In 1978, the good-looking Prince, now a major in the Royal Hussars, married the daughter of an Austrian nobleman, Baroness Marie-Christine von Reibnitz, who is now titled Princess Michael of Kent. As the new Princess is a 35-year-old Catholic divorcée, the marriage to Prince Michael encountered two formidable obstacles. First, under the 1701 Act of Settlement, a member of the royal family who wishes to remain in the line of succession cannot marry a Roman Catholic. This barred the ceremony from being performed in an Anglican church. Second, even if the

Princess had renounced her Catholicism (which she didn't), the Anglican Church doesn't allow a church wedding for divorced persons. The couple was eventually married in a civil ceremony in Vienna, with the private support of the bridegroom's family. Prince Michael had to renounce his rights to succession, but any children of the marriage will not have to do so provided they are baptized in the Church of England. To date, the reception given from the British press and public to the charming Princess Michael has been overwhelmingly favorable. Their first child, Lord Frederick Windsor, was born in 1979.

As will be explained more fully in the chapter on royal titles, the designation of Royal Highness does not extend to the children of any of the marriages of these cousins of the Queen, nor of course does it extend to the husband of Princess Alexandra. The oldest son of each of the royal ducal marriages will inherit his father's peerage, but as nonroyal dukes. The daughters and younger sons of these grandsons of a king are styled Lord or Lady, the "Lord" and "Lady" appearing before their first names. The rule applies whether or not the father is a peer (that is, a royal duke); hence, any children of Prince Michael of Kent will be titled Lord or Lady. In the fourth generation descended from the sovereign (King George V), all will be plain "Mister" or "Miss" Windsor, except for the lines inheriting the dukedoms.

Closer to the Queen is her only sister, Margaret. Four years younger than Elizabeth, Princess Margaret Rose (she dropped the second name during the War as "childish") was England's sweetheart—the nation's noncinematic Shirley Temple—during her teens and young womanhood. Since the middle fifties, she has been more accurately characterized as the most difficult member of the family.

The difficulties began with an internationally famous love affair with Peter Townsend, dashing ex-RAF officer and

World War II hero, and an aide to the Princess's father. Townsend had made a hasty wartime marriage and was only recently divorced. The sanctimonious public opinion of the time, as well as the even more sanctimonious Church, demanded that Margaret break off her relationship with Townsend. In 1955, she issued a public statement to the effect that she was doing just that. The official reason was that a marriage between the two would go against the "teachings" of the Church of England—an institution which her sister was sworn to "defend"—and would thereby damage the Crown. If Margaret had married Townsend she would also very likely have lost her State allowance and official position (though not her title). Presumably, Elizabeth finally persuaded her to give up Townsend (at the alleged insistence of the Duke of Edinburgh, an interference, according to some reports, for which Margaret has never forgiven Philip), but the Princess's chances of ever inheriting the throne made all the hullabaloo fairly absurd. The Queen's two children stood between Margaret and the throne, and she wouldn't even have served as regent for a minor Prince Charles in the event of her sister's death—that thought so filled Parliament and the Court with horror that Philip had been named to replace Margaret as regent-designate. (It is unusual for this position to be filled by someone other than a person in line of succession to the Crown, which Philip was in only an extremely distant way—like his wife, he was also descended from Queen Victoria, but in a line distantly removed from any possibility of inheriting the Crown.) The kicker is that it is by no means certain that Townsend ever actually asked Margaret to marry him.

Perhaps on the rebound, Margaret fell for Antony Armstrong-Jones (she accepted his proposal on the night she learned that Townsend was about to marry someone else), a young and well-connected professional photographer and semi-aristocrat (after divorcing his father, Tony's mother married the Earl of Rosse), and married him in 1960. While awaiting the birth of their first child, Armstrong-Jones was prevailed upon to accept a peerage, the earldom of Snowdon, a maneuver solely designed to save the child from the ignominy of being a titleless nephew of the Queen. This son, David, was born in 1961 with the courtesy title of Viscount Linley, his father's second title, and will someday inherit the earldom. A second child, born in 1964, is Lady Sarah Armstrong-Jones.

Margaret is a strange personality. She wants to be one of the gang, until someone actually treats her as such, when she instantly remembers who she is and reverts to being strictly royal. Dare anyone, including intimate friends, call her anything other than "Ma'am," she will immediately freeze the offender with her inimitably imperious glare. Her nickname, "PM," is, needless to say, used by no one to her face. Only members of her family are allowed to call her Margaret. Britain's jet set satirically refers to her as "Yvonne."

The Princess's marriage started to go bad rather early. Her husband bridled at the public deference which protocol required he pay her, as well as at the more serious restraints that marriage to the Queen's sister placed on his career in commercial photography. Even granting Margaret's less than even temper, allowance has to be made for the unusual circumstances of her life. She was born second fiddle, and has had to live a lifetime in the shadow of her sister. It is understandable that a person in such a position would want some serious attention to be paid to her. Margaret is obviously extremely fond of being a princess, and wouldn't consider the alternative for a split second, but she must nevertheless sometimes feel at loose ends.

Her husband lost sympathy for her fairly soon, and started a life of his own away from the luxurious living quarters in Kensington Palace that his sister-in-law had given the couple as a "grace and favor" residence. Their widening rift

turned into a separation in March 1976, and a divorce two
years later. Snowdon soon remarried, to 37-year-old Lucy
Lindsay-Hogg, the daughter of an Irish dress designer, on
December 15, 1978; it was also her second marriage. In October 1979, the Earl's daughter by Princess Margaret became
a godmother to his new daughter, Lady Frances. Lord and
the second Lady Snowdon live in an £85,000 house not far
from Kensington Palace. Snowdon, who has no inherited
wealth, lives on his comfortable income from a career in photography, including royalties from his books of photographic
essays.

While being criticized by a good part of the world's
press, Margaret was unable to make any statements explain-
ing her view of matters. Members of the royal family simply
don't defend themselves publicly against criticism. If while
still married she had begun a relationship with a rich (brewery
heir), young (17 years her junior) ex-hippie and singer
manqué, Roddy Llewellen—with whom the Princess is now
seen frequently in public—then it should be remembered that
for many years the earl had been connected publicly with
other women.

Margaret still captures world press headlines, but those
headlines are now usually critical, controversial, or both. A
recent imbroglio was the result of an allegation that she had
referred to the Irish as "pigs." The setting was a cocktail
party in Chicago, where she was on a tour of American cities
to raise money for the Royal Opera House at Covent Garden. Even though she could be sympathized with for her
feelings—her cousin Lord Mountbatten had recently been as-
sassinated by Irish terrorists—such a comment from the
Queen's sister is extremely ill-advised in our age of ethnic
tensions. The Princess, through her secretary, of course de-
nied she said anything of the kind, this despite the affirmation of Chicago's Mayor Jane Byrne that she had. In any
event, American IRA sympathizers made a shambles of the

remainder of her trip, including turning a pig loose—presumably an Irish one—at a San Francisco reception in her honor.

Now 50, Princess Margaret has become a matronly middle-aged woman with a face that leaves no doubt of having been around the block. But she is still the Queen's only sister, and millions of people are intensely interested in her every movement. It is possible that she may yet strike a happy balance between being a princess and a woman.

If people could have their choice of a grandmother, there is little question that many would choose someone exactly like Queen Elizabeth The Queen Mother. (The term "Queen Elizabeth" refers to the Queen Mother; the term "the Queen" refers only to her daughter, Queen Elizabeth II.) Queen Elizabeth is Britain's Grandmother Compleat, a universally loved and respected dumpling of a woman. Much of her storehouse of goodwill can be attributed directly to a remarkable personality combining royal dignity with just the right mix of good-humored friendliness.

Born Lady Elizabeth Bowes-Lyon in 1900, she was the youngest but one of the 10 children (and today the last survivor) of the Earl and Countess of Strathmore, wealthy holders of an ancient Scottish peerage. She was reared in two homes. St. Paul's Walden Bury, the family's English redbrick Georgian country home in Hertfordshire, is the idealization of a splendid mansion of the British aristocracy. The Scottish home, where Elizabeth was born, is the Glamis (pronounced Glahms) Castle in which Macbeth supposedly lived. The castle, near Dundee, has been owned by the family since the 14th century. In addition, the Strathmores had a London townhouse first in St. James's Square, and then at 17 Bruton Street, Mayfair, where Elizabeth's first daughter was to be born. Although the young Lady Elizabeth would become Britain's first queen not of royal birth since Anne

Hyde (daughter of the Earl of Clarendon) in the 17th century, she nonetheless came from a background of privilege and high position, good training for her distinguished future role.

In 1923, Elizabeth married the second son of King George V. This marriage, which simultaneously made her a royal highness, a princess, and Duchess of York, was not expected to have dynastic implications. Her husband's older brother was heir to the throne, and in the normal course of events she and Bertie would have been able to lead lives at least partially private. Instead, the couple became King and Queen, and never again was any part of their lives truly private.

Queen Elizabeth's honored place in her country's history is the result of two significant contributions. The first is the support—beyond calculation—that she gave her husband as king, especially in the difficult early years after his accession. George VI was a shy man afflicted with a bad stutter; his health was frail and his temperament was volatile, in large part because of his inability to express himself without stammering (which in turn was most likely the result of his martinet father's constant hectoring and quarterdeck behavior toward him as a child and young man). Elizabeth's presence literally made it possible for him to carry on, encouraging him especially in difficult speaking engagements.

Her second legacy was the image she projected, which, together with the King, inspired the British people during the War. Seemingly everywhere at once, she brought warmth and sympathy to thousands of bombed-out Britons. Refusing to flee to safety even during the worst of the Blitz, she remained a symbol to her countrymen, and has reaped their deepest affection for it ever since.

On her husband's death in 1952 when she was only 51, she supported her older daughter by fulfilling many public duties, putting all of her many qualities at the new Queen's disposal as she had for her husband. At the same time, she was helping Margaret through her affair with Peter Townsend, then building toward its culmination.

The Queen Mother has in recent years reduced her public role, befitting a woman now 80, but she still gets out to her favorite charity bazaars, film and stage premières, annual events such as the Chelsea Flower Show, and an occasional tour abroad. She was recently named Lord Warden of the Cinque Ports, a symbolic honor, but succeeding such illustrious incumbents as the Duke of Wellington, Sir Winston Churchill and Sir Robert Menzies.

Short and stout, with incredibly tiny feet, her preference in apparel has always run to frills and furbelows, huge wide skirts in her own robe-de-style fashion (which King George VI loved her to wear), and generally with as many of her fabulous jewels as possible. Inevitably, she looks like a Christmas tree. Turned out thus, she is the Queen Mum the world expects her to be.

Queen Elizabeth lives in Clarence House, the pale cream Georgian mansion just down the Mall from Buckingham Palace. Her charismatic presence permeates every corner of the great house. It is said that even the cleaners at Clarence House feel lonely when she is away. Her main country home, the Castle of Mey, is a small crenellated château on the northernmost tip of Scotland. She bought the house in the early sixties, and has since restored it to a perfect state. The Queen Mother's Windsor home is The Royal Lodge in Windsor Great Park, which she occupies nearly every weekend. When staying with her family at Balmoral from the end of August until the third week in October every year, she uses Birkhall on the estate.

An interesting point concerns the Queen Mother's title. Had Mrs. Simpson been allowed to marry King Edward VIII and become Queen, and assuming a childless marriage, as it turned out to be, the present Queen would have still come to the throne, but in 1972 on Edward's death, and as a middle-aged woman of 46. And her mother, rather than being Her Majesty Queen Elizabeth The Queen Mother, would have remained Her Royal Highness the Duchess of York, the Queen's mother. There's a world of difference between Queen Mother and Queen's mother.

The Queen's husband is a man who, had he not married the Queen, would now probably be heading a major international corporation, if not a country. Philip was born in 1921, the son of an obscure Greek prince far down his country's line of succession to the throne, and an Anglo-German princess who was the great-granddaughter of Queen Victoria. He was blond, good-looking and a scion of Danish, Russian, but mostly German royalty by blood (many of the Danish and Russian monarchs having taken German princesses as their queens) but without a drop of Greek blood, a country whose dynasty was descended from the Danish royal house. Reared from his early teens by his uncle, Lord Mountbatten (his mother's brother), and Lady Mountbatten (daughter of Lord Mount Temple and granddaughter of Edward VII's financial adviser and close friend, Sir Ernest Cassel), he brushed around the edges of royalty all his young life. Philip joined the Royal Navy—his uncle's influence—and served during the War, acquitting himself a genuine war hero.

When Elizabeth fell in love with Philip, the flaxen-haired Greek prince wasn't thought a particularly grand catch for the heiress to the throne. During their courtship in the years immediately following the War, Greece was embroiled in a civil war, pitting Communists against Royalists. Britain's governing Labour Party didn't much want to approve the marriage of even a remotely possible heir to the Greek throne into the British royal family, especially to the King's heir. Furthermore, King George felt his daughter hadn't had a chance to shop around, that her attention to

Philip might merely be the infatuation of an immature and unsophisticated girl.

But Elizabeth and Philip's ardor was genuine. Her father consented to the match, and they were married in a resplendent State ceremony in Westminister Abbey in November 1947. Philip continued his naval career and, in Elizabeth's only real whiff of leading anything resembling a normal existence, they lived fairly simple lives together at his duty station in Malta in 1950.

At this time, between her marriage and her accession to the throne, Elizabeth's title was "HRH The Princess Elizabeth, Duchess of Edinburgh," as her husband had been created Duke of Edinburgh immediately preceding their marriage. On her accession, even though her husband remained Duke of Edinburgh, she ceased being his duchess, the principle being that the sovereign is the fount of honor and can hold no inferior title of nobility (except that of Duke of Lancaster, a title held by either a king or queen regnant).

Two children were born, Charles in 1948 and Anne in 1950. But with the King's increased debility from cancer and phlebitis, Philip's active sea service had to be terminated so that his wife could serve as a full-time stand-in for her father. On the King's death in February 1952, when Elizabeth was 25 and Philip 30, their lives underwent a drastic change. Although they had planned a large family, the new monarch's time-demanding duties would not permit any more children for many years.

Philip's problem was just the opposite of the busy Queen's—he had too *much* time on his hands. The British constitution makes no provision for a regnant queen's consort; his only recent British role model was Prince Albert. As could have been foreseen, Philip's main mission came to be one of supporting his wife and relieving her of many of the second-rank obligations which she found difficult to fulfill, and sharing with her the private function of head of their own family and household.

It is often said that while Philip publicly defers to the Queen, at home he brooks no interference from anyone, including his wife. Such speculation is an exaggeration. The royal family can't be considered truly private even inside its cocoon. The national role the Queen plays can't be turned off at home; decisions affecting their children's education and many other domestic concerns require the Queen's full participation and approval. There is little doubt that the Queen defers as much as possible to her husband, sensitive to his feelings and to the general notion of the place of a man in the family, but it stretches credulity to suggest that she is in any way less than a full partner in their private lives.

Although it is a role his son is rapidly usurping, Philip is still his country's leading pitchman for homemade goods—in a manner befitting his dignity, of course. He can be exceedingly abrasive and sarcastic to functionaries however (to a dignitary waiting on a red carpet to greet him, "Do you like standing here? Is it what you usually do on a Monday?"), and has come in for withering press criticism for the "get the finger out" toughness he uses in his campaign to modernize British industry. He is involved with nearly 400 organizations, mostly in the position of honorary patron. Philip is also the chancellor of two universities, Cambridge and Salford. (Most members of the royal family hold the position of chancellor at one of Britain's universities—Princess Anne at the University of London, Prince Charles at the University of Wales, the Duke of Kent at the University of Surrey, the Duchess of Kent at the University of Leeds, Princess Margaret at the University of Keele, and Princess Alexandra at the University of Lancaster; mighty Oxford has a former prime minister, Harold Macmillan, filling the role.)

For many years, Philip was an ace polo player. Because he is now approaching 60, he has given up the sport, and has let his eldest son become the family polo star. His new sporting occupation is carriage-driving, even more a rich man's hobby than polo.

In his major dynastic duty, that of producing an heir, he has performed splendidly. All things considered, it is difficult to see how Elizabeth could have picked a man better able to fulfill the role of consort—one which holds no official place or precedence. Philip—or "Keith" as he is satirically known in Britain in counterpart to his wife's "Brenda"— could have been a leader in his own right. Instead, his real function has been to *support* the leader, regardless of any independent achievements. That he is one of the most popular public figures in Britain, and would stand an excellent chance of being the first president of a Republic of Great Britain, speaks well for his success.

Prince Charles Philip Arthur George is the Heir Apparent to the British Throne. On his mother's accession in 1952, he automatically became Duke of Cornwall, Duke of Rothesay, Earl of Carrick, Lord of Renfrew, Lord of the Isles, and Great Steward of Scotland. In 1958 he was created Earl of Chester and at the same time given his most important title, Prince of Wales. He has since been made a knight of the Garter, Thistle, Bath, and the other British orders of chivalry. Thirty-two years old in November 1980, Charles is a peer of the realm, a distinction not yet shared by his younger brothers. Only the sovereign's eldest son is heir to these titles; mere birthright as a prince does not confer status as a peer.

The Prince of Wales has evolved into an extraordinary man. The British people were fortunate, considering the chances of a person born into his position turning out to be mediocrity or worse. An international celebrity since his birth, Charles seems to be everything anybody could want in an heir to the throne. He is handsome, jug ears notwithstanding, and a smashing dresser. He is intelligent, charming beyond belief, and has acquired completely the requisite royal art of always appearing to be interested in whatever he's being shown. He inherited his grandmother's remarkable charm and her ability to make a person feel he is the sole object of genuine royal concern. In short, he is the consummate prince, and so much a popular symbol to Britons that he is said to be at the top of the IRA's hit list.

Schooled at Cheam and his father's alma mater, Gordonstoun, where he was a "late bloomer," Charles enrolled at Trinity College, Cambridge, to study anthropology and history, knowing full well he could never follow a career in either field. In 1969, during his Cambridge student days, he was invested as Prince of Wales at Carnarvon Castle. One of the most colorful events of the Queen's reign, although not universally popular with the Welsh, this ceremony marked Charles's real passing into manhood. The investiture was mired in controversy over Welsh nationalism. In an attempt to blow up some local government offices, two separatist-minded terrorists blew themselves up with a homemade bomb which went off sooner than scheduled. Charles's coolness and grace throughout the tense time earned him great acclaim.

After receiving a Master of Arts degree in 1970, the Prince entered the Royal Navy as a midshipman, leading to his own first command, of the minesweeper HMS *Bronington* in 1976. (During his naval service, he was known officially as "HRH Lieutenant The Prince of Wales," but was addressed by the men on his ship as "Lieutenant Charles Windsor"; to his superior officers he was simply "Wales" while on duty—but the moment he stepped out of his role as a naval officer to be a prince again, even admirals were obliged to call him "Sir.") At the end of that year, Charles left the navy as a commander; if extended, the career would have impinged on his duties as heir to the throne.

His first civilian job was to head the committee planning his mother's Silver Jubilee celebration. Today, in addition to his heavy load of ceremonial duties, he works with young dropouts and keeps a hand in other areas of social welfare. So far, the Prince's greatest success has been the Silver Jubilee Appeal (an offshoot of the Jubilee itself), a drive which collected £16,000,000 to be used for grants for youth self-help programs. A typical grant was given to renovate an ambulance for young first-aid trainees.

His chief assistant is his Private Secretary, Edward Adeane, the great-grandson of Lord Stamfordham (Queen Victoria's and King George V's private secretary) and son of Lord Adeane (the Queen's former private secretary), and a one-time page at Court. The new secretary, a bachelor, gave up a thriving practice as a libel barrister in 1979 to take the prestigious job in the Prince's suite. Prince Charles's secretary for many years, RAF Squadron Leader David Checketts, left royal service that year after 18 years at the palace. At the age of 50, a mild friction with the Prince set in, caused innocently by Checketts's continued over-fatherly treatment of his young employer. The former pilot's leaving was by mutual consent. Adeane is Charles's age and was the Prince's own appointment (as Checketts was not), and thus should be far more controllable, and therefore more to Prince Charles's liking.

Long before he succeeds to the throne, Charles will probably be given high flag rank in all three of the armed services; on succeeding to the throne, he will become an Admiral of the Fleet, Field Marshal, and Marshal of the Royal Air Force. In his case, these honorifics will have at least been partially earned by his active service, unlike the passing out of high rank to many princes of the past. (The Duke of Windsor retained his field marshal status even after his abdication. When he was assigned to the staff of the British commanding general in France during the early days of World War II, this rank created an awkward situation vis-à-vis his new commanding officer, so the Duke magnanimously relinquished it, on a strictly "temporary" basis, for that of major general.)

On February 23, 1981, the Queen announced her eldest son's engagement. As had been rumored in Britain for months, Charles would marry Lady Diana Frances Spencer, the youngest of three daughters of the 8th Earl Spencer, a wealthy Northamptonshire landowner. The summer 1981 ceremony would be the first wedding of an Heir Apparent to the British Throne since 1863 when Charles's great-great-grandfather—the future King Edward VII—married Princess Alexandra of Denmark.

Like his maternal grandmother, the Prince's bride is a member of one of Britain's great noble families—in Lady Diana's case, the Spencers are interrelated with numerous other peerages, including the Abercorn duchy, the Fermoy barony, and even, although distantly, with the Churchills and the Marlborough duchy. Lady Diana's father, Lord Spencer, is the eighth holder of an earldom dating from 1765; his mother was a daughter of the Duke of Abercorn. After Eton and a stint in the Royal Scots Greys (rising to Captain), he served as an equerry to both King George VI and the present queen, succeeding to the earldom in 1975. In 1954, he married the Honorable Frances Roche, a daughter of the 4th Baron Fermoy. Their marriage was dissolved in 1969. The present Lady Spencer, Raine, is the daughter of novelist Barbara Cartland; Lady Diana's mother also remarried and is now Mrs. Peter Shand-Kydd.

Diana's status takes an astronomical leap with her marriage. As Princess of Wales, the beautiful young English-woman will rank a mere notch below the pinnacle of British society, with the only other women preceding her being the Queen and the Queen Mother. Her introduction to royalty, however, is not of recent vintage. Lady Diana, who was born in 1961, grew up at her father's leased country home, Park House, on the Queen's Sandringham estate. As a child, she was often in the company of the royal children; the Prince of Wales taught his five-year-old future consort how to swim. Her older sister, Lady Sarah, who at one time dated Charles herself, described the engagement as "perfect—they are both over the moon about it." Throughout her paparazzi-plagued courtship with Charles, Lady Diana exhibited good humor and patience, fine harbingers for success in the harrowingly difficult new role she has to fulfill.

It's a safe prediction that Charles will be Prince of Wales for many more years. The chances of his mother's abdicating are nil, and her health can only be described as radiantly good. But there is little doubt that the Queen will continue to involve Charles to an ever-increasing degree in the heavy workload she carries. The result will be that England will have the best of both mother and son—a wise and experienced sovereign, and supporting her an attractive and popular heir able to be active in many areas unreachable or unsuitable to the monarch.

Her Royal Highness The Princess Anne, Mrs. Mark Phillips, is the second of Elizabeth and Philip's four children. Born in 1950, Anne is very much her father's daughter. Often rude and not infrequently downright coarse, she has made at least one genuine achievement—she was named Britain's Sportswoman of the Year in 1972 (for show jumping "contributing to British sport") and was a member of the British equestrian team at the 1976 Olympics in Montreal.

Schooled adequately, at Benenden in Kent, Anne discovered her only real love in horses, a fondness which great wealth makes so practical. Many contend that given her unusual opportunities, any young woman could rise to a high level of prominence in riding, but the argument is hollow. Anne's talent and skill are real and painstakingly achieved. More likely it is *because* of her unique position that she has worked so hard to rise to an international championship level in riding, a way of demonstrating real excellence, the kind that Princess Margaret, for example, has never tried to achieve.

In November 1973, Anne married Mark Phillips, a

young officer in the Queen's Dragoon Guards and the maternal grandson of one of King George VI's aides-de-camp. Phillips's looks might have served as the model for a recruiting poster. The couple met through their mutual interest in horses, Captain Phillips being a world-class rider in the same league with Anne. One of the riding activities they still share is fox hunting, for which they are constantly criticized by the Hunt Saboteurs Association, a group which agitates against hunting "small wild animals." Another activity they share is the constant breaking of Britain's highway speed laws. Both have been booked for the offense. Phillips's brother-in-law, the Prince of Wales, reportedly isn't overly fond of him; according to one biographer Charles calls him "Fog"—short for "thick and wet."

Their first child, Peter, was born in 1977. Peter Phillips is one of the few legitimate grandchildren of any modern English sovereign born without a title. The only other instance in the last 400 years was the second son of King George V's daughter, Mary; even that child, Gerald Lascelles, was born with the style "Honorable," at least making him something more than just plain "Mister."

In the spring of 1978, Captain Phillips left the army to concentrate on farming, and took a year's training course at the Royal Agricultural College to enable him to take over the operation of the 750-acre Gatcombe Park estate the Queen had bought the couple as a wedding present. The Queen owns another 600 acres at the adjoining Aston Farm, and the two acreages are now being farmed together. The reason for Phillips's leaving the army was a practical and realistic one—as a member of the royal family, he would have been unable to serve in areas of potential danger, such as Northern Ireland. With the competition for promotion so high in Britain's shrunken officer corps, those without front-line experience are unlikely to attain advancement.

The Princess's husband came in for a serious trashing in the British press in October 1979. The incident arose from

what he evidently considered to be an innocent business deal
with British Leyland. However, the *Spectator* pointed out
several seriously damaging issues which unfortunately
emerged out of the ill-considered deal.

British Leyland, Britain's last major producer of automobiles, offered to sponsor Phillips's team of show jumpers
to the tune of £60,000 over three years. The money was to
help pay for the upkeep of the horses and to get them ready
for the 1980 Olympics. Phillips's part of the bargain would
be to "sponsor" the Land Rover, the one vehicle in BL's
stable which still makes money for the near-bankrupt company. Phillips himself would receive no hard cash in the arrangement; to have done so would have meant the loss of his
amateur status, which would leave him ineligible for the
Olympics.

Normally, such a deal would be above criticism. Except
that in this case it, one, further besmirched the already be-
leaguered amateur ideal in the Olympics; and two, the company involved was trying to persuade thousands of its
employees to accept voluntary termination as the alternative
to its collapse.

The first issue was the least offensive. The amateur ver-
sus professional controversy at the Olympics has already become a matter of complete hypocrisy. The only regret was
that a member of the royal family should have participated
at all in the funerary rites of the Olympic amateur ideal. Of
more importance was the fact that the deal with British Leyland should have come at a time when the company was
pleading near insolvency and when thousands of its workers
would be laid off with little likelihood of finding jobs in Britain's ossified auto industry. To hand over £60,000 to a member of the royal family to help him continue to jump his
horses was a bitter pill for the company's work force.

But the greatest potential damage was that done to the
royal family itself. When questioned about the propriety of
the deal, Phillips replied, "We have a mortgage like everyone

else." In fact, the Queen *gave* Anne and her husband the £750,000 estate; the mortgage is one the Phillipses took out to improve the stables with a heated footbath for the horses. Since Gatcombe Park yields about £50,000 annually, with the Princess pulling down a yearly £60,000 Civil List (State allowance), the poor-mouthing went over with a dull thud. The royal family, including its members by marriage, is not in the business of advertising products. If Mark Phillips didn't realize this, his wife should have.

The two youngest and least-known members of the Queen's immediate family are Prince Andrew, born in February 1960, and Prince Edward, born in March 1964. As children, Andrew and Edward were kept out of the public eye to such an extent that people began to wonder if they were all right. Andrew has grown into an astonishingly good-looking young man, so popular with the girls that he is familiarly known as "Randy Andy." Like his father and older brother, he was schooled at Gordonstoun. After graduating in May 1979, he skipped university and immediately joined the Royal Navy, a traditional career for younger sons of the royal family.

In September, Andrew was posted as a midshipman for six months at the Officer's Training College in Dartmouth. It soon became apparent, at least to the press, that Andrew's popularity at the college wasn't as high as that of his father and brother as cadets. According to classmates, the Prince likes to remind people often and forcibly of his royal rank, a trait not designed to win friends. As one unnamed courtier said, "Andrew as king would be like Margaret as queen—it would put us all out of business." Even though he signed up for a 12-year hitch, as the Queen's son he will be expected to fulfill many nonnaval ceremonial obligations. The Prince anticipates becoming a helicopter pilot as his service specialty.

One of the advantages of being the Queen's son is the car Andrew drives. The German-built Ford RS-2000, a car which will cruise at well over 100 m.p.h., was a gift from his mother. Andrew's driving is said to give his bodyguard, Scotland Yard Inspector Steven Burgess, whose youthfulness almost matches Andrew's, moments of extremely taut nerves. Few 20-year-olds in Britain have this kind of car since most insurance companies won't touch them, and any that do set premiums at over £1000 a year.

For the time being, he signs his exam papers at Dartmouth "Midshipman HRH The Prince Andrew," but if his mother follows a well-established tradition, he'll be made Duke of York soon after turning 21. The title has been borne many times by the second son of the English monarch. So far, it has never carried down to a direct second generation, the holders either unexpectedly inheriting the throne or else dying childless. Both Kings George V and George VI were Dukes of York. As a royal duke, Andrew will become a peer of the United Kingdom and thus a member of the upper house of Parliament.

Edward, the youngest member of the family, is also the quietest of the Queen's children. His blond hair and amiable demeanor are reminiscent of his late great-uncle, the Duke of Windsor. Edward is now at Gordonstoun, where he has academically outpaced his father and brothers. Unlike Andrew, Edward's scholastic aptitude will probably ensure that he'll go to university. A number of ducal titles have been suggested for the prince's majority; a likely choice is Duke of Sussex.

Sixteen years separate Charles from Edward; the two younger sons were much like a second family for Elizabeth and Philip. But the family is still intensely close-knit, partly because it is impossible for any of them to really let loose with outsiders. As a result, the Queen and her husband, their sons and daughter and son-in-law, together with Princess

Margaret and her children and the Queen Mother, are together for many extended periods throughout the year, carrying on the traditional royal role of serving as the nation's
model family.

Finally, there is the senior member of the family—the
Queen. Elizabeth II is the most famous, most photographed
and most curiosity-arousing person in the world. She has
been the subject of countless biographies and millions of
words of print. Arguably, she is the richest woman on earth;
very few men are richer. She leads the life of an ancien ré-
gime grandee, one that nobody else anywhere quite comes
up to. She lives in the world's most sumptuous palaces and
travels on the world's largest yacht. She is Queen and Head
of State not only of the United Kingdom, but of 10 other
countries as well, and is Head of the 36-member Commonwealth (a formula devised after World War II to keep countries antagonistic to the idea of monarchy from dropping out
of the fraternity). She is head of all of Britain's armed services and orders of chivalry, as well as secular leader of the
Church of England. Her collections of jewelry and art are
genuinely breathtaking and literally beyond price. She stands
outside the law, as opposed to all others of her subjects. To
conspire against or even to think of any injury to her person
constitutes high treason. She is the fount of honor in Britain,
and she is anointed and consecrated in a job from which
there is no planned retirement. As if all this weren't enough,
she is, in her mid-50s, still a most attractive woman, a genuine authority on horse breeding, very happily married, and
a whiz-bang at crossword puzzles.

The Queen (she is never called "Queen Elizabeth") has
her work precisely cut out for her. She takes great pride in
a thorough knowledge of what's going on in her kingdom and
in the world. She meets with the Prime Minister every Tuesday evening when she's in London, and is briefed on domes-

tic and foreign affairs and matters before Parliament. Her famous "boxes," strongboxes brought round to the palace from Whitehall, are crammed with all sorts of State documents, most of which she reads verbatim. Any bills enacted by Parliament are enclosed, and her signature on them will make them law.

While the Queen's only real rights under 20th-century constitutional monarchy are to advise and to be advised (or as the historian Bagehot put it in the 19th century, "the right to be consulted, the right to encourage, the right to warn"), it must be remembered that she has outlasted seven prime ministers, always keeping fully abreast of major political and governmental activities. In spite of her hothouse upbringing—similar to that of a novice in a covent, more comfortable but nearly as cloistered—the Queen is a woman of at least average intelligence and well-above average common sense. For a prime minister to ignore out of hand a warning or suggestion from the Queen would be unwise, and British politicians know it.

The Queen's very real constitutional role aside, her greatest job is being *seen* as Queen. Elizabeth understands the symbolic importance of this, and has gone to great lengths all her life to make sure that her actions and behavior have been worthy of emulation. Criticism of the Queen has been extremely scanty, not just out of loyalty to the concept of the throne, but because there has been precious little to criticize in this monarch. She simply doesn't mess up.

The Queen's passionate interest and relaxation centers around horses. She owns valuable racehorses, and knows their breeding histories inside out. Four days after her coronation, she was enjoying herself immensely at her Coronation Derby. At one time—during the late fifties—there was some barely concealed grumbling in the country that the Queen appeared to care more for her horses and race activities than for her subjects. Since then, her public participation in equestrian events and the public's tolerance for it have both mellowed.

Elizabeth is paradoxical in one respect—there is nobody else about whom so much is known, and yet only a handful of people know her personally, that is, *really* know her and how she thinks. The Queen doesn't much like to be in the news, and, oddly, works very hard to stay out of it. The trivia about her in the realm of common knowledge is vast. It's been reported that her skirts have lead weights sewn into the hems to keep them from flying up in breezes. Her love affair with corgi dogs is legendary, leading many to call the BBC-TV program about her family life "Corgi and Beth." When she's angry, knowing persons can tell because she twists her wedding ring around her finger. She wears half-glasses for reading, but is very rarely photographed with them on. Yet the Queen has never given an interview, never answered a criticism. She's never publicly given a political opinion. Her friends call her Ma'am, her mother, sister and husband call her Lilibet, and *nobody* calls her Elizabeth. The Queen has a profound belief in the God-granted nature of her position. A friend once remarked to her that King George V's notorious rudeness could be returned as well as received. Her instant response was, "Not to the King—you can't be rude to the King." In turn, and because of this, the Queen is never discourteous and seldom peremptory to others, knowing full well they would have no recourse but to accept it.

This distance is exactly what the Queen wants. Besides a natural disinclination to "show," she knows she is never a person apart from her position, and it is this position that she regards as an absolutely inviolable trust, deserving and demanding dignity and respect. It is also this attitude which renders any suggestion of eventual abdication in her son's favor as extremely unlikely.

2

Shelter
THE ROYAL RESIDENCES

London, midmorning, midweek. It's threatening to rain, or maybe the humidity is finally getting ready to coalesce. About 75 tourists—average for a "nonevent" day—are clinging to the ornamental fence in front of Buckingham Palace, carefully scrutinizing any movement at the windows. The biggest knot of people has gathered around the bobby at the north gate of the great pile's east front—the facade seen in a million photos of this the most unknowable famous building in the world.

Behind the gate, the corporate headquarters of Her Majesty Queen Elizabeth II is humming along at full tilt. The 40 housemaids and 50 footmen are waging a barely winning battle to keep the place presentable, but their trade union makes sure they aren't treated like their predecessors in the prewar royal establishments. The clock-winder, who does nothing else, goes about his repetitious rounds. A corps of bureaucrats, the chief daytime occupants in terms of numbers, do what bureaucrats do everywhere: draw up and carry out schedules, calculate accounts, see to importuning outsiders, take their tea breaks.

But all these royal employees, from courtiers to labor-
ers, are special, and they're aware of it every moment. Their
employer is also their nation's personification of authority,
whose face graces every coin, every banknote and every postage stamp in the kingdom, and whose existence embodies
the sum of 53 generations of sovereign kings and queens.

Buckingham Palace is of course the epicenter of royal
Britain. Just a few hundred yards down the Mall is Clarence
House, home of Queen Elizabeth The Queen Mother. The
house itself is a small palace attached to a larger palace—that
of St. James's. The latter is still the official diplomatic seat of
the Court, and every ambassador and envoy to the United
Kingdom is accredited to the Court of St. James's.

Verdant public gardens stretch back from Buckingham
Palace's own park-sized private grounds, through Hyde
Park, Kensington Gardens—until one reaches Kensington
Palace, still very much a royal residence, housing cousins
and a sister of the Queen.

Down Birdcage Walk stretching through St. James's
Park in front of "Buck House," as the royal family calls its
chief residence, is the Palace of Westminster, where the
Queen's ministers and legislators make the laws which govern, and sometimes misgovern, Britain. Even Westminster is
still officially a royal palace, and thus under the aegis of the
Crown. Oddly, it is the one royal palace the Queen can't
legally visit without an invitation.

At the other end of the capital is the oldest of Britain's
royal palaces, the Tower of London. In reality now only a
museum and repository for the Crown Jewels, it remains officially a royal residence, where every night the ceremony of
the Queen's Keys is enacted with great drama and pomp.

What strikes the visitor to the sprawling city is how
royal it in fact is. Although the monarch's participation in the
governing of her country is now symbolic, her presence in
the everyday life of the country is still pervasive. While
much of Britain has gone to seed, anything on which the

label "royal" is hung is always briskly scrubbed and neatly clipped.

One universal truth about British royalty is that they live well—exceedingly well. When it's reported that some royalty or another is living in "modest" or "unpretentious" circumstances, this should not be understood in the usual meaning of those terms. The truth is that royal figures dwell in settings that were designed to emphasize their apartness from ordinary folk. When, for instance, King George VI wished to escape from the cares and grandeur of his several main residences, he could always retreat to The Royal Lodge, a place the royal family loved for its "coziness and charm." Before you imagine that this Royal Lodge was a vacation cabin, it should be pointed out that the mansion is on a par with a good-sized resort hotel, although infinitely better furnished.

This chapter will describe the many residences of the royal family—their palaces in London as well as the country estates and castles which they regard as their real homes. We'll start with the world's grandest palace still functioning as a royal home, and describe in detail this royal city within a city.

BUCKINGHAM PALACE

Buckingham Palace is the only royal residence in the world named after a nobleman, in this case the duke who built the nucleus of today's structure. The history of the site—which King George V liked to say was in Pimlico, the déclassé and distinctly unroyal neighborhood bordering on the south—goes back into the earliest records of this part of London.

The *Domesday Book* of 1086 records a Manor of Eia which was bounded on the west by the river Westbourne, the east by the river Tybourne (these are still in existence, but now flow under the city, emptying into the Thames; the Westbourne surfaces briefly in Hyde Park's Serpentine), the Thames on the south, and what is now the Bayswater Road and Oxford Street on the north—then the Roman road from London to Bath. The manor, at that time owned by the abbots of Westminster, would survive intact for nearly 900 years as a part of the Grosvenor estate, except for that portion which became Buckingham Palace and Hyde Park. Much of the original estate is still owned by the Grosvenor family—the Dukes of Westminster—including Eaton Square, Grosvenor Square with its American Embassy, a third of Mayfair, the south side of Oxford Street, and all of Belgravia. The only major loss has been Pimlico, which the family had to sell off after World War II to pay "death duties"—inheritance taxes which have broken up most of Britain's great estates.

The Manor of Eia, covering about 1,100 acres, wasn't worth very much when the abbots owned it. The main problem was that it was subject to continual flooding, and was in reality just a great swamp. Even the origins of the names of the surrounding districts refer to this flooding. Where the land rose above the flood level, the areas were called islands, or "ea." Thus Bermonds'ea—the isle of Bermond; Chels'ea—the isle of Chesil; Batters'ea—the isle of Batriches, or Patrick's Isle.

The manor was finally taken from the monks in the mid-16th century by Henry VIII in his "Dissolution of the Monasteries." Henry's motivation for this thieving, which was carried out on a grand scale all over England, was to break the power of the church for its refusal to grant him a divorce from the wife who hadn't been able to bear him a son.

The abbots didn't have anything of great value on the land—the chief building was the leper hospital of St.

James's. Henry threw out the lepers and turned the hospital into a hunting lodge, the forerunner of St. James's Palace. He later had the land to the west drained and enclosed, and laid it out as a pleasure garden, called St. James's Park.

Henry's daughter, Queen Elizabeth I, used this inheritance from her father very carefully. Whereas her father had given away chunks of it to favorite courtiers, she kept the greater part attached to the Crown and made grants only of short-term leases as a form of compensation for services rendered. Less judiciously, her successors—James I, Charles I and Charles II—reverted to the old practice of giving away large slices of the land. As a result, under James I and Charles I the recipients, now independent of court favors, did much to help the Parliamentary cause leading to the Commonwealth. But the Crown presciently kept the parts on which would be built today's palace and its gardens.

King James I tried to start a silkworm farm on the site, but because the wrong type of mulberry tree was imported— silkworms don't much care for the leaves of the black mulberry tree, preferring the white—the venture failed. A pleasure ground was operated in the place of the mulberry gardens, and it is said that the first cup of tea brewed in Britain was drunk there. Nothing more was done on the site until after the Restoration of the monarchy under Charles II.

The first documented building to stand where Buckingham Palace is located today was called Goring House. In the first decade of the 17th century, the land around what is today's palace was entirely country; the centuries-old development of London had completely ignored this still marshy part of Westminster, and except directly around St. James's, the areas surrounding Goring House would not be built on until the 19th century.

George Goring, Earl of Norwich, was a favorite in the court of Charles I. The King gave him the failed mulberry farm, upon which the Earl proceeded to build his home,

Goring House. During the Cromwellian interlude, his statement, "Had I millions of crowns and scores of sons, the King
and his cause should have them all," endeared him to the
exiled Charles II, but had cost him his new home and almost
cost him his head on a republican block. A restored and
grateful Charles returned to him the land which the Round-
heads had taken from him. At his death three years later, the
house (located where the present palace's northern wing today stands) and land came into the hands of the Earl of Arlington by way of a 99-year lease given him by the Crown,
and it quickly became the capital's society magnet. When the
old Goring House burned to the ground in 1674, Lord Arlington rebuilt the mansion on a far grander scale, naturally
renaming it Arlington House. On his death, his daughter
and son-in-law, the Duke and Duchess of Grafton (the Duke
was one of the many illegitimate sons of Charles II, in his
case by the Countess of Castlemaine), inherited it, but the
soon-widowed Duchess found it too big for her reduced
means, and she rented it to the Duke of Devonshire.

In 1703, the mansion again burned to the ground, and
the Duchess sold the ground lease to the Duke of Buckingham. For clarity's sake, it should be pointed out that this
Duke of Buckingham was not related to the earlier two
Dukes of Buckingham (father and son), the first of whom
governed England under James I, the latter performing a
similar function for Charles II. This line died out, and the
title was reconstituted on John Sheffield, Earl of Mulgrave,
who was promoted to a dukedom and for whom today's royal
palace is named.

Buckingham became one of the great Tory powers of
Britain under Queen Anne, and on her death in 1714 he was
one of the Lord Justices who ruled the country until the ar-
rival of King George I from Hanover. His new residence,
which he built in 1703 and named Buckingham House, was
one of the greatest town mansions in the nation, far better

than anything the royal family lived in. Its orientation was exactly that of today's palace—facing east, with a long garden frontage on the west side. Its vantage point looking down the Mall (then a long grassy field ending at Charing Cross) was the most impressive in London, another fact not lost on the royal family. The Duke's new house was to last just over a century—until 1823.

The Duke died in 1721, and was survived by his Duchess, a natural (the nice way of saying illegitimate) daughter of James II (brother and successor to Charles II) and who considered herself very much a royal "personage." Because of her parentage, the house became a hotbed of Jacobite plotting and counterplotting to restore the deposed Catholic line, with vast sums of money being spent on these clandestine activities. Her only son, Edmund, predeceased her, so the property passed on her death in 1742 to Charles Herbert, the illegitimate son of her husband the late Duke. The Buckingham title thus became extinct for the second time, and the new owner had neither the means nor the inclination to keep up the semi-regal court which Buckingham House had become during his father's day. In 1762 he sold the remainder of his lease of 11 years to King George III who in turn gave it as a dowry gift to his new Queen Charlotte. Buckingham House finally became a royal palace.

Although St. James's Palace and Kensington Palace were retained for ceremonial occasions, Buckingham House was now the de facto seat of the monarchy and government, and by contemporary accounts, Their Majesties were very happy in their new home. No particularly big changes were made on the mansion itself, but new gates were put up, the stables in what is now Buckingham Palace Road were enlarged to include a riding school, and the ground-floor library was enlarged to accommodate the King's favorite hobby, book collecting. The couple lived a quiet life, animated by their brood of 15 children, the bearing of which took place from 1762 to 1783. The last was born five days before the coming of age of the first, the Prince of Wales.

George III lived until 1820, the last 10 years quite mad and totally blind, and during which time his son served as Regent. It was this son to whom today's palace owes its existence.

"Prinnie," as the profligate and debauched George IV was known during his long apprenticeship and regency, was one of the 19th-century's big spenders. Since he didn't have to be concerned about earning the millions of pounds he cajoled out of Parliament, he had absolutely no conception of the value of money, except that it took a great deal of it to do his bidding. His Oriental pleasure palace at Brighton, built when he was Prince of Wales, had cost £750,000, this when a pound bought perhaps 20 times more than today. During his earlier years as King, the re-creation of Windsor Castle, from a hodgepodge of medieval buildings to the grandest castle in the world, had taken place, giving him good preparation for the impressive work to come on Buckingham Palace.

Immediately after his coronation, he started drawing up plans for a suitable city palace, something he evidently didn't consider his magnificent Carlton House to be. The rebuilding of Queen Charlotte's dower house received its first serious consideration a year after her death in 1818. Parliament set a limit of £150,000 to be spent on the new palace, a sum the new King found to be laughably inadequate. The finished residence would actually cost over £720,000 (a figure arrived at through creative bookkeeping) before anybody would ever live in it.

By 1825, the actual work began. John Nash, the architect who had recently completed the Regent Street and Regent's Park developments, designed a palace which retained the shell of the old Buckingham House exactly as it was, while adding space for the Household. The now familiar east front was not at that time anticipated, and the palace was basically U-shaped, with long wings on either side built out toward St. James's Park. On the Mall front, a two-storey portico of coupled Corinthian columns was designed as the Grand Entrance. (It survives today unaltered, but alas unseen because of the enclosing east wing.) The original scheme did produce a partial quadrangle effect with the erection of the Marble Arch in front of the palace. The old wings of Buckingham House (the north and south wings) were pulled down, and new ones built farther out, with colonnaded screens running outward at right angles from their ends, screens which also are still in place today. The main front—today's west wing—contained all the state rooms on basically the same lines of the former mansion.

Much of the palace's furnishings came from Carlton House, including parquet flooring, scagliola (plaster painted to resemble marble) columns and wood carvings. The wily King hid much of the value of the riches going into the palace by showing only the expense of moving them from one to the other, thereby hoodwinking more money out of Parliament for more furnishings—thus the creative costing of the palace. Nash later estimated the value of the fixtures from Carlton House at £13,601 18s 6d—a figure intimating the precise character of the architect's mind.

When George IV died in 1830, the palace was structurally complete, but the interior unfit to live in. His successor, William IV, refused to have anything to do with it, even suggesting it be turned over to Parliament after the old Palace of Westminster burned in 1834. Nash, who would die in 1835, had been replaced in 1831 by another architect, Edward Blore. Blore made several changes in Nash's work, most notably doing away with the much ridiculed dome Nash had put over the garden front. In 1835, King William was persuaded to announce his intention to live in the new palace (rather than remaining at Clarence House, the residence he and his consort Adelaide had inhabited since they were Duke and Duchess of Clarence), and in May 1837, the building was finally ready for him to occupy. The King died the next month, never having made it.

Three months after her accession, Queen Victoria, with her mother the Duchess of Kent at her side, drove in state from her girlhood home of Kensington Palace to her new home. The transformation from Goring House to Buckingham Palace was finally complete.

But it wasn't long before Victoria started making changes. Her marriage to Prince Albert in 1840 gave her an excuse to evict her mother, who was occupying the eastern half of the private (north) wing. (The Duchess of Kent went first to live in Belgrave Square before moving into Clarence House on the death of King William's widow, the Dowager Queen Adelaide.) By 1845, Queen Victoria was complaining to the Treasury that she was "suffering great inconvenience from the insufficient accommodation afforded by the palace," this apparently in the light of her growing number of children. This incredible protest led to the final major construction of the palace.

Unfortunately, Mr. Blore was again chosen to carry out the alterations. The resulting new east wing, which transformed the U-shaped building into a hollow square and would forever hide the old Grand Entrance in the new quadrangle, was decorated in about as ugly a manner as possible, completely desecrating the classical beauty of Nash's work. *The Builder*, in its issue of August 18, 1847, said that it "looked like little more than an ordinary piece of street architecture." During these alterations, the south wing was also redesigned, with a huge new ballroom built over the kitchens in the southwest corner. In reality, the need for a larger chamber in which to hold the grand balls so beloved of Queen Victoria was probably the real reason for her wanting the palace enlarged, rather than her ingenuous wail that "our little family is growing up." A fortuitous secondary effect was to have even more important results. The plumbing and drainage arrangements, which had been a source of noxious fumes and vermin at the palace since Victoria first moved in, were greatly improved during this period of reconstruction.

The final alteration carried out at the time was the removal of the Marble Arch from in front of the palace, which if left in place would have been hard up against the facade of the new east wing. It was moved to the northeast corner of Hyde Park, and has given its name to the adjacent tube station and surrounding neighborhood.

When Albert died in 1861, the palace went into a 40-year dust-sheet phase. During her four-decade-long self-imposed purdah, Victoria rarely visited London, preferring the isolation of Windsor, Balmoral and Osborne. But with her son's accession in 1901, it once again became the real as well as official seat of the monarchy and court.

Only one significant exterior alteration has been made since Blore enclosed the courtyard. The east facade—the main front—was redesigned and refaced by Sir Aston Webb in 1913 to serve as a "fitting background" for the new Victoria Memorial which was built in 1912 to terminate the palace end of the Mall. In order not to disturb the existing archways or windows—the wish of King George V—Webb designed a simple neoclassical facade in Portland stone, replacing Blore's crumbling Caen stone. The latter is still visible at the southeast corner of the palace, a sort of pinkish color contrasting with the gray of Webb's facade.

Today, Buckingham Palace is the one royal residence instantly identifiable by millions of people all over the world. It is to this great squat mass of stone-covered masonry that half of London gathers for those watershed moments in British life—coronations, royal births and deaths, wars beginning and ending. In the center of the facade facing the Mall, nestled between fat columns on the second floor, is the most famous balcony in the world. Here the Queen and her family show themselves to the massed crowds which have gathered outside the gates and sometimes spill down the Mall past the Queen Mother's Clarence House. It is on these occasions that the magic of Buckingham Palace is most evident, and it becomes the focal point of the largest freely associated commonwealth of mankind in history.

The palace is a square with a large central courtyard. There are three main storeys, for which it is easier to use the palace's official nomenclature of ground, principal and bedroom floors rather than deal with the confusion between what the British would call the ground, first and second floors and what Americans would call the first, second and third floors. Above these is a smaller attic floor. About half of the total space of the palace's 600 rooms (no two people agree on an exact number, but this figure serves as a convenient approximation) is occupied by the splendid state and semi-state apartments (what lesser people call rooms) and their connecting corridors, a fourth is taken up by Crown and Household offices, and something less than the remaining fourth represents the private apartments of the royal family.

The ground floor of the east wing is broken up by the arched openings which correspond to the gate openings in the ornamental iron railings surrounding the graveled forecourt. The large center gateway and arch are used only on State occasions; the Queen normally enters by a side gate on the north wing. Looking at the palace from the Mall, the entrance on the right side of this east facade is the Privy Purse Door, used by business visitors to the palace. There are flats on this floor for the palace Superintendent and

Housekeeper, as well as various records and personnel offices. The corridor on all floors of this wing, as well as the north and south wings, give entrance to rooms on one side only (except for part of the north wing's ground floor), looking inward to the courtyard; only the corridors in the west wing open onto rooms on both sides.

The most famous room on the east wing's principal floor is the Balcony Room, exactly in the center of the palace's main facade. This room from which the royal family emerges onto the renowned balcony was decorated by Queen Mary in a kind of weird but expensive Chinese manner. The newly completed balcony itself was first used by Queen Victoria in 1854 when she watched battalions of her troops march out of the forecourt before leaving for the Crimea. The Principal Corridor extends for 240 feet along the whole length of the floor, segmented into three sections by mirrored doors and crosswalls, and serving today basically as a gallery in which to display works of art. Blore filled the east wing with many of the best fittings from the Brighton Pavilion, the seaside palace which Victoria would no longer use after Albert had Osborne House in the Isle of Wight built for her.

On either side of the Balcony Room are semi-state suites, the northerly being the Buhl Room Suite (formerly the Empire Suite) ending at the north corner in the Chinese Luncheon Room, the southerly the Blue and Yellow suites for state guests, ending at the south corner in the Green Drawing Room.

Prince Charles's suite is on the bedroom floor of the east wing, with his windows overlooking the Mall and St. James's Park. His combined sitting room-study, bedroom and bathroom are in the southeast corner. There are also bedrooms for ladies-in-waiting to the Queen at this end of the corridor. The room directly over the Balcony Room has been used in the past as a classroom for the royal children, including the latest generation; directly above it on the roof the Royal

Standard flies whenever the Queen is in residence at Buckingham Palace. Farther along this corridor to the north are bedrooms used by visiting private guests of the royal family. Above the east wing is an attic floor of small rooms for staff and storage.

The north wing overlooks Constitution Hill (a street, not a hill) and across from it Green Park. It is the main preserve of the Queen and Prince Philip. Each has a large suite off the King's Corridor on the principal floor, containing a sitting room-study, bedroom and bathroom. These rooms really constitute their private "flat," and are never open to anybody but family and intimate friends.

Since the palace kitchens are a quarter of a mile away in the south wing, food usually came lukewarm to the royal table, so Philip installed a small kitchen in their "apartment." But tradition dies hard, and the new kitchen is little used. Instead, electric trolleys now bring the food from the old kitchens. (The Queen, by the way, does not cook. Even if she had the inclination, she certainly doesn't have the time.)

The sanctum sanctorum is the Queen's sitting room. Located toward the garden front, it has the only bow window on the north facade, which easily identifies it in photographs. Her bedroom is next door toward the east, followed by her dressing room. The next several rooms are the Duke's, and they stretch almost to the Chinese Dining Room overlooking the Mall. The royal couple's dining room is next to the Queen's sitting room on the west, nearly at the garden end of the wing. Even though their private quarters take up only a small part of the palace, the Queen and Prince Philip can hardly be considered cramped.

The bedroom floor of the north wing includes rooms for Prince Andrew and Prince Edward (the northeast corner rooms) as well as private guest rooms and servants' quarters. Bobo Macdonald, the Queen's Dresser, has a two-room suite directly over her mistress's suite. Next door is a huge room, lined in cedar, which serves as the closet for the Queen's wardrobe. Miss Macdonald is in charge of this vast selection of some of the world's most expensive clothes, and keeps it all in filing-cabinet order. The chests holding the Queen's jewelry are kept here as well. One of the most affecting scenes in the "Royal Family" film showed the Queen, sitting with Miss Macdonald, casually fingering a piece of jewelry worth a zillion pounds, wondering "Have I worn this before?"

Completing this floor toward the west are the store-rooms and maids' rooms. As with the other wings, there is a small attic floor above the bedroom floor.

The ground floor of the north wing is primarily made up of offices. The door at the eastern end is the Privy Purse Door, opening onto the forecourt. Immediately to the right inside this door is a small room where anybody who wishes to do so may sign the Visitor's Book, a fact not overly pub-licized in fear there'll be a steady queue down the Mall of those waiting to get even this tiny glimpse of the inside of the palace. The next room is a good-sized chamber where visitors with appointments to see a member of the Household are asked to wait. For the first-time visitor to the palace, waiting in this elegant little room gives a hint of the greater splendors to come. On one wall is the famous Frith painting, *Ramsgate Sands*, a fascinating tableau of mid-Victorian seaside holiday-makers. Its placement probably wasn't a random choice in that it has the power to absorb the viewer for some time. Under the painting is a table on which the morning *Times* and *Telegraph* are laid out—the two daily papers one supposes are most relevant to this most exclusive of settings. Incidentally, until recent years a special edition of *The Times* was printed on silk rag for the monarch's personal use. Must have been a lovely touch.

Continuing down the Privy Purse Corridor are the offices of the Keeper of the Privy Purse, the Queen's Treasurer, the Queen's Private Secretary, and the Press Secretary
to the Queen, as well as areas for clerks and typists, footmen,
equerries, a small library and a small emergency surgery.
None of these offices displays much of the grandeur of the
rest of the palace. The bow-shaped space under the Queen's
sitting room on the floor above is the royal family's entrance,
inside and across the corridor from which is the Queen's elevator. A large attached pavilion jutting off the west end of
the wing contains a swimming pool, which is much used by
the Prince of Wales.

The least-known wing—the south wing—is basically a
service and staff wing, with one great state chamber, the
Ballroom, on the principal floor's west end. At the forecourt
end of the ground floor is the Visitor's Entrance, used by
social visitors. The Lower Corridor, the main ground-floor
passage, opens onto Household offices on the left, including
those of the Prince of Wales's Office. Farther along are the
immense kitchens and offices for the domestic staff. The police have a small office here, and the colonnaded screen jutting out at a right angle from this wing houses a post office
and guardroom. The impressive-looking entrance on the
street side of the south wing is called the Ambassadors' Entrance (formerly "The Entrée") and is the portal for foreign
representatives on their way to present their credentials to
the Queen. In older days, the sovereign gave permission for
really important persons to enter the palace through this door
on State occasions, thus avoiding the common herd entering
through the Grand Entrance.

The only public part of the palace proper, the Queen's
Gallery, is at the west end of the ground floor, but the public
reaches it through a tunnel-like corridor from an entrance in
Buckingham Gate, the road bordering the palace on this side.
Absolutely nothing of the architectural majesty of the palace

itself is evident in a visit to the Gallery, a small and contemporarily decorated room and mezzanine built at the order of the present Queen on the site of the palace chapel which was bombed during the Blitz. The exhibits in the Gallery are changed periodically, and generally represent the finest elements of the vast royal collection. A recent exhibition featured the works of a single artist, the court painter Hans Holbein.

The south wing's principal floor is used mostly for staff offices. The Master of the Household has a large office overlooking Buckingham Gate, the vaguely tatty thoroughfare (which becomes Buckingham Palace Road just north of the Mews) running past the palace from the Mall to Victoria Station. Toward the west end of this floor, adjoining the Ballroom, is the State Supper Room, a mid-Victorian chamber used now for late evening buffets for guests in the Ballroom.

The Ballroom is, at 60 feet by 123 feet, the largest room in the palace, and is used for the grandest of State occasions, including banquets for visiting heads of state and investitures. The room was designed and built in 1854 by Sir James Pennethorne, adopted son and pupil of Nash. With its pair of thrones on a raised dais surmounted by a lush crimson canopy (made for the 1911 Durbar in Delhi) with a huge gold crown surmounting it, the whole affair recessed in a gold-and-white marble pilastered enclosure looking down the giant chandeliered chamber, the inescapable effect is one of deliberate and awesome majesty.

Finally, there is what was designed to be the central part of the palace, the west wing, with the rooms on its east side looking out into the courtyard over the Grand Entrance, those on the west side overlooking the palace gardens. In it are contained the magnificent state and semi-state apartments.

The double-colonnaded Grand Entrance is seen only after passing through the triple-arched entrance from the forecourt into the quadrangle. The quadrangle, or central courtyard, is itself a completely lifeless space, devoid of any greenery or fountains. One doesn't enter directly through the center of the Grand Entrance, which is covered with a glass screen, but instead through one of the two rather pokey doors on either side. The shallow flights of steps lead immediately ahead to the Grand Hall, which is backed by a set of eight wide steps. At the top is the 20-foot-wide Marble Hall, traversing the entire wing. The Grand Hall and Marble Hall, while suitably impressive with their gilt, cream and scarlet decoration, are unusually low and "squashed" in proportions. Many of the mansions of the nobility which once dotted London had vastly more regal entrance halls; even the still-surviving Lancaster House across the Mall makes Buckingham Palace's entrance look almost puny by comparison.

To the right off the Grand Hall are the two small Stamp Rooms where successive monarchs have kept up the world's most valuable stamp collection. (Stamps were something of a mania for George V. His biographer, Harold Nicolson, said that all the man did was "kill animals and stick-in stamps.") To the left is the aptly named Grand Staircase which ascends in an awe-inspiring spatial complexity to both the principal and bedroom floors. Directly ahead, across the Marble Hall, is the Bow Room, the room most seen by social visitors to the palace since guests at the Queen's garden parties pass through it to the portico leading onto the gardens. The red-draperied and carpeted room, with its bow-shaped bank of five double French doors, was at one time the palace library, and it is where Queen Victoria held meetings of the Privy Council, including the one at which she announced her intention to marry Prince Albert. During World War II, when the private apartments were uninhabitable because of bomb damage to the windows, the Bow Room was used as a sitting room by the royal family.

Opening on the south side of the Bow Room is the '55 Room, so-called from the year of its remodeling in the 19th

century, and which is today used as the Household dining
room. Adjoining it on the south are the Household breakfast
room and the Queen's cinema. To the north side of the Bow
Room are the '44 Room (remodeled in 1844 in honor of a
visit from the Russian czar) and the five-room group known
as the Belgian Suite for Victoria's uncle, King Leopold of the
Belgians, though he was only the first in a long and glittering
line of kings and emperors who have been put up in this
luxurious set of rooms. The Queen and Prince Philip use the
'44 Room for private luncheon parties, and here the Queen
receives letters of credence from foreign ambassadors and
holds meetings of the Privy Council. The Belgian Suite was
used as his private apartment during the few short weeks that
Edward VIII lived at Buckingham Palace as King. (Queen
Mary didn't vacate the palace until October 1936, nine
months after her husband's death and during which time the
new king continued to live at York House in St. James's Palace. King Edward probably realized by October that his
term as king wasn't going to last very much longer, and
opted not to have the normal private suite in the north wing
redecorated for him.)

The most monumental part of the palace is the west
wing's principal floor. The best way to describe it is to take
a round trip from the north end adjoining the private apartments.

The Royal Closet is the smallest of the state rooms. The
room is by no means a "closet," the term a holdover from
more spacious days. Actually it's a small and exquisitely furnished drawing room. It is in this room that the royal family
congregates on State occasions before making their always
impressive entry into the rooms where the guests are assem-
bled. (The area on the north side of the Royal Closet, at the
juncture of the north and west wings, is a part of the private
apartments; the room immediately next to the Closet on the
north is the Queen's Audience Room.) The Royal Closet
connects with the next apartment, the White Drawing

Room, through a secret door concealed by a swinging pier glass and table, the effect of which is predictably stunning to the guests as the Queen comes floating through this almost magical grand gadget. The White Drawing Room, a fantasy in white, gold and crimson, is famous as the setting for many royal photographs and portraits since King Edward VII and Queen Alexandra's time. The chandeliers, like those in several other state apartments, at one time hung in Carlton House, the long-vanished palace which once stood in Carlton House Terrace.

Twelve-foot-high doors lead into the next chamber, the Music Room, also bow-shaped, corresponding to the Bow Room directly below it. The Music Room is perhaps the most theatrical of this range of state rooms, decorated in crimson and gold, the high-domed ceiling supported by 18 extraordinary scagliola columns the color of lapis lazuli. The piano, still played by members of the royal family, belonged to the Prince Regent. Family christenings are held here (the last for Peter Phillips), and after World War II it served as a temporary chapel.

Next on the axis is the Blue Drawing Room which served as a ballroom for a young Queen Victoria before architect John Pennethorne built her the bigger one. At the end of this line of rooms is the State Dining Room, created for George IV, whose portrait together with those of other Hanoverian royalties surround the room. The chamber is used for smaller State dinners (larger ones taking place in the Ballroom), private banquets and large family parties. The Spanish mahogany dining table, which looks like a fair-sized skating rink thanks to its glossy surface, can seat 60 diners when fully expanded with its eight leaves. Conversation is difficult though, since the table is eight feet wide—shouting across to the Queen isn't done. It was in this room that an unfortunate lady of Queen Victoria's Household told of having seen a notice that the "Duchess of Atholl" (a coach) left the "Duke of Atholl's Arms" (an inn) at 7:00 each morning, the joke at which Queen Victoria was first to be recorded as being "not amused."

The Dining Room leads, via the West Gallery, into the Ballroom. Two routes can be used to head back in the direction from which we've come: through the Ballroom and then the East Gallery, or by the Cross Gallery connecting the East and West Galleries. Either way, we go through the principal floor's connecting corridor, the Picture Gallery, corresponding to the ground floor's Marble Hall, and which separates the rooms facing the gardens from those which overlook the quadrangle. The Picture Gallery has no exterior walls but is lighted from a huge curved skylight running the entire length of the ceiling. The many masterpieces in what amounts to the palace's private art museum are individually illuminated by strip lighting. There are five chimney pieces around the gallery, a reminder of the days when fireplaces furnished the palace's only heating system. (Central heating wasn't installed in the palace until after World War II; many rooms still have space heaters installed in the fireplace openings.)

On the quadrangle side off the Picture Gallery are the three final state apartments. The Guardroom serves as an anteroom to the Green Drawing Room. The gloriously rich little chamber has no other particular function, except perhaps to dazzle. The Green Drawing Room is directly over the Grand Entrance of the floor below and is the assembly point for those entering the apartment on the north, the final state room, and the very heart and center of the British monarchy.

No kingdom can be without a Throne Room, a place where His or Her Majesty can sit on a great gilded chair and be regal. Hundreds of movies have shown it so well. Nowadays, the Throne Room at Buckingham Palace has yielded its function to a great extent to the State Ballroom, also having a throne dais, but the red silk-and-gilt chair at its end is still considered the Throne of England. The chair was built as the Queen's Chair of Estate for her coronation in Westminster Abbey. Joining it on the dais is a matching throne for Prince Philip, his embroidered with the initial "P," while the Queen's has her cipher emblazoned on it. The huge crystal chandelier, surrounded by six smaller ones, is now wired for electricity and its light equals that of nearly 3,000 candles. Close to the dais is the only other "secret door" in the state apartments. The Queen uses it to return to the private apartments after State functions.

The gardens of Buckingham Palace in reality constitute a medium-sized private park in the heart of London, about the same dimensions as the public Green Park across Constitution Hill directly to the north. The palace and its gardens are surrounded by six streets—Buckingham Gate, Buckingham Palace Road, Lower Grosvenor Place, Grosvenor Place, Duke of Wellington Place (at the Hyde Park Corner apex of the roughly triangular site), and Constitution Hill; the palace itself faces the west end of the Mall—which the British pronounce to rhyme with "gal," not "wall."

The 39 acres contain the largest grassy lawn in the United Kingdom as well as a five-acre lake fed by the river Tybourne, long diverted underground. The whole establishment is surrounded by a wall (except for the railing at the forecourt) with a particularly nasty-looking revolving spiked railing on top, installed by Prince Albert to thwart such episodes as the Boy Jones's uninvited visits to Queen Victoria. The wall is something of a tantalizer to the London pedestrian who feels shut out from an inviting urban glade.

There are about two and a half miles of gravel paths, all of uniform width, through the gardens, now used as a royal jogging trail, especially by Prince Charles on his morning

exercise sessions. Although the gardens contain every imaginable kind of plant and tree that is suitable to London's cli-
mate, including a swamp cypress, they have no fountains or
statues, something rare for a royal palace's setting. The most
famous ornament on the grounds is the Waterloo Vase, a 15-
foot-high marble urn commissioned by Napoleon in Tus-
cany, and presented to King George IV after Waterloo.

Other than the Queen's Gallery, the only feature of the
palace complex much known to the public—unless the guests
at the Queen's garden parties can be considered "public,"
which is doubtful—is the Royal Mews, located along the palace's south wall, where Lower Grosvenor Place becomes
Buckingham Palace Road. The derivation of the word
"mews" is interesting, especially since it has nothing to do
with the idea of stables or garages, the modern meaning of
the word. It comes from the Old French "mue" (from the
Latin "*mutare*," to change), meaning a change, especially of
an animal's coat or skin. A "mews" in the Middle Ages was
a place where the king's falcons were kept during their
"mewing" or change of plumage. For many centuries, the
king's mews were in what is now Trafalgar Square, on the
spot where the National Gallery stands today. Until the
reign of Henry VIII, only falcons were kept there, but when
the royal stables in Bloomsbury burned, Henry removed the
falcons and used the mews solely for his horses.

The Riding School in the present mews was built by
Nash when Buckingham House was occupied by George III.
In 1826, the school became the nucleus for the new royal
stables, moved from the Trafalgar Square site. Today's
mews consist of a quadrangle entered from Buckingham Palace Road through a Doric archway surmounted by a clock
tower. The east side of the quadrangle consists of garages for
the collection of state carriages; the stables for the Queen's
horses—some of the finest horse lodgings in existence—are
in the north and west wings. On public display is the state

harness, a massive display of the gorgeous collection of bits, snaffles, collars, reins and hundreds of other trappings used to caparison the Queen's horses on State occasions. Most are made of dazzlingly polished brass, some are gold-plated, and all are crafted like fine jewelry.

Buckingham Palace is off limits to visitors, except for the Mews and the Queen's Picture Gallery. The palace is listed in the phone book, though, in quite ordinary small type; the number is 930-4832. The chances are very remote that even the state apartments will anyday soon be open to sightseers. (It has actually gotten more exclusive over the years. In the early part of Queen Victoria's reign, more "genteel" elements of society could buy tickets from the Lord Chamberlain to stand in the Grand Hall and Grand Staircase to watch the Queen process on her way to the State opening of Parliament at Westminster.) The Queen has already opened to the public several rooms of her private home, Sandringham, and the democratization of the monarchy might lead one to imagine Buckingham Palace's eventual accessibility. It is, after all, one of the world's great repositories of treasure, and was paid for by the British people—and their former subjects. But the Queen's Assistant Press Secretary, when queried on the subject, cataloged a long list of real and imagined difficulties which make the palace's opening unlikely. Much of the building is, in effect, an office building, albeit a highly unusual one. Even the state rooms are in fairly constant use by the Queen for entertaining and ceremonial purposes. There is only a skeleton staff on duty on weekends, and its augmentation in order to allow sightseers would be extremely expensive considering the high cost of labor. In the Queen's principal period of absence, summer, the palace is thoroughly cleaned and repair work done. Finally, the press spokesman stated that 90 percent of the art treasures in the palace have already been put on public view, mostly via the Queen's Gallery.

Nobody pretends, of course, that the public's primary interest in Buckingham Palace is to see the pictures or the objets d'art. What people want to see is *where the Queen lives*— how the rooms are arranged—the actual places they've heard about all their lives, so mysterious behind the gray facade, seemingly reserved forever for the few privileged enough to be the Queen's guests, a category of which the vast majority can never hope to be a part.

WINDSOR CASTLE

In recent years Windsor Castle has become the weekend retreat of the royal family. Both far enough from London to seem somewhat removed from its pressures and close enough for the Queen to attend to her official duties, Windsor has proved an almost perfect second home for Elizabeth and Philip. The "almost" is because the castle's one drawback is that the landing path of London's primary airport, Heathrow, goes directly overhead. Presumably, the three-foot-thick walls keep the worst of this annoyance from royal ears. In any event, it is the residence the royal family considers "home."

Windsor Castle's gray battlements rise majestically above a chalk hill on the Berkshire bank of the river Thames, 25 miles west by southwest of Buckingham Palace. Situated right on the edge of the commercial heart of the city of Windsor (officially "New Windsor"; the hamlet of Old Windsor is two miles southeast of the castle), it is Europe's largest surviving castle and the most imposing royal castle in existence.

Seen from the air, Windsor Castle looks something like a large boomerang. It is divided into two main sections: the Lower Ward, with St. George's Chapel, and the Upper

Ward, the "palace" part with the state and private apartments. The two halves are connected by the smaller Middle Ward with its Round Tower at the juncture of the boomerang.

The place now called Windsor didn't exist before the building of the castle, and the "Windlesora" ("winding shore") for which William the Conqueror named his new fortress refers to the town of Old Windsor. The spot was chosen because of the commanding chalk heights which overlooked the Thames, then the country's primary commercial artery. William built the castle in the then revolutionary "motte and bailey" design, which boggled the minds of the semi-civilized Anglo-Saxons whom he had so lately subdued. The central feature was the "motte," a large flat-topped earthen mound topped by a wooden fortress and encircled by a ditch. This area was surrounded by the "bailey," a larger walled area where men and animals could take refuge and shelter could be built. The whole thing was surrounded by a moat.

Nothing is known of the first royal living quarters within the timbered structure, but by 1110, King Henry I started holding court in the castle's Upper Ward, probably along its north flank overlooking the Thames Valley. Within its first century of existence, the basic division of the castle was set: the Upper Ward serving as the sovereign's residence and the Lower Ward accessible to the public for its religious and ceremonial rites. The same holds true today.

Late in the reign of Henry II, the wooden structures in the compound were replaced with stone walls and buildings. The lower half of the Round Tower as well as the outer walls of the Upper Ward date from this late-12th-century period.

Within the next century, the castle was besieged twice, something that hasn't happened since. Both sieges had to do with the malevolent King John, nemesis of the legendary Robin Hood. The second rebellion, the more serious of the two, finally ended when John died and was succeeded by his son, Henry III. Henry kept building new battlements, their circular outlines distinguishable from the square ones built by his grandfather—military experience had shown during the years between grandfather and grandson that structures without corners were harder to knock down.

A century later, King Edward III founded England's premier order of chivalry at Windsor—the Order of the Garter. To provide a worthy setting for it, he demolished Henry III's buildings, and built new and more spacious apartments. He converted the Lower Ward to serve as the Order's headquarters. A chapel was built, but 100 years later King Edward IV began the building of the present St. George's Chapel, replacing the older structure. The chapel, named after the patron saint of the Garter, is today one of the most famous surviving examples of the perpendicular Gothic style and one of the world's greatest ecclesiastical buildings. It was completed during the reign of Henry VIII in 1528.

It is also to King Henry VIII that the south side of the Lower Ward owes its appearance. He had the lodgings for the clergy converted into apartments for the Poor Knights, a group of retired soldiers of limited means which was established by Edward III in association with the Order of the Garter. Henry provided in his will for a permanent company of 13 such knights, whose successors, renamed the Military Knights by William IV in 1833, still inhabit these quarters.

By the reign of Charles II in the 17th century, the essentially medieval royal apartments in the Upper Ward had become irredeemably uncomfortable, so he commissioned the architect Hugh May to rebuild them in the fashionable baroque style, the basic structure of which survives as today's state apartments.

At this time, the King laid out the three-mile-long avenue of elms known as the Long Walk. Bordered by elm trees which stood for nearly three centuries before having to be felled in 1945 owing to disease, the Long Walk runs straight south from the Upper Ward's private apartments, past the city of Windsor, and into the Great Park.

After another century (during which time most sovereigns chose not to live at Windsor), another king decided to undertake a really grandiose reconstruction of the castle. George IV's vision of a proper setting for a monarch was nothing if not majestic, and it was during his reign that the Upper Ward was turned into the sumptuous palace that has been home to every king and queen since.

The architect chosen by George to do the work was Jeffry Wyatt, a brilliant and theatrical man. His royal patronage so inflated his self-esteem that he petitioned the King to be allowed to change his name to the more elegant Wyatville; the impatient George snorted, "veal or mutton, it makes no difference so long as he finishes quickly," and then bestowed a knighthood on the architect to help prod him along. The changes made by Wyatt, now Sir Jeffry Wyatville, gave Windsor the glorious profile we see today when viewing the castle from a distance. He integrated the confused jumble of buildings into a whole, changing the plain walls into mock-Gothic crenellated battlements with many new towers around the castle's perimeter. The most dramatic exterior change was to raise the height of the Round Tower by building it up by 33 feet, enough so that it commands and unifies the castle's 13-acre site. (At 102 feet by 95 feet, the Round Tower should really be called the Oval Tower.) Wyatville also created the magnificent state apartments which are now filled with some of the world's greatest art treasures.

Victoria and Albert spent many happy years at Windsor, and it was here that the Queen passed much of her widowhood, secluded within its heavy walls. Edward VII and George V moved their courts to the castle annually for rounds of ceremonious festivities, but both preferred Buckingham Palace and Sandringham. Edward VIII didn't much care for the place because of unhappy boyhood memories, but will always be associated with it for the moving abdication speech he read to the world from its Augusta Tower.

During World War II, the castle was home for Princesses Elizabeth and Margaret, whose bedrooms were safely located in the bombproof Lancaster Tower. Their parents spent as much of their time there as possible during the war years, the King finding relief from the strain of London by indulging his fondness for gardening.

In the present reign, Windsor has become, after Buckingham Palace, the major residence of the Queen and the Duke of Edinburgh. Besides spending most weekends there, in June the Queen plays host to a five-day house party during Ascot Week. Windsor has now supplanted Sandringham as the royal home where Christmas Day is spent.

The "palace" half of the castle in the Upper Ward is almost overwhelmingly magnificent. The state apartments in the north wing are open to the public; the private apartments and the Queen's private suite in the east and south wings are not. The visiting public can enter the castle's Upper Ward through either the Norman Gate on the north side or St. George's Gate at the base of the King Edward III Tower, the latter leading to a path which winds along to the north side where the entrance to the state apartments is found. The quadrangle is closed, together with its State Entrance; sightseers enter through the Public Entrance in the King George IV Tower on the North Terrace.

Straight ahead inside the Public Entrance is the base of Wyatville's Grand Staircase, which ascends to the principal floor and its range of state apartments accessible to the public. The beauty of the staircase itself has been badly marred by the building of a "temporary" wooden bridge across it which serves to separate entering sightseers from those exiting. Even though these areas are usually swarming with tourists, it should be remembered that when the Queen is in *official* residence (all of April and several other weeks throughout the year), the state apartments serve the purpose for which they were built, being used extensively for formal entertaining by the royal family, and thus are closed to the public.

The first state apartment at the top of the Grand Staircase is the Grand Vestibule, filled with cases of military uniforms and weapons, the latter extending up the walls in splendidly intricate designs of crossed rifles and pistols and bayonets in huge circles. Enormous double doors lead into what is Windsor's most famous room, the Waterloo Chamber, built by Wyatville over an open courtyard which originally filled the area. The Chamber is the scene of an elaborate banquet which takes place every June 18 to commemorate the Allied victory over Napoleon, and in which the current successor to the Duke of Wellington is the Queen's guest of honor. (A recent menu: cold avocado soup, salmon, veal in cream sauce with new potatoes, baby carrots from the Windsor gardens, spinach salad, pineapple ice cream in hollowed-out pineapples with sponge fingers, and a different wine with every course.) Around the room is the famous series of paintings by Sir Thomas Lawrence of the monarchs, statesmen and warriors who played the major roles in defeating Napoleon. The immense table surrounded by 70 chairs (those seated at either end are nearly invisible to each other) rests on the largest seamless carpet in Europe, made in India for Queen Victoria.

Leaving the Waterloo Chamber, one enters the Garter Throne Room, another example of Wyatville's lavish touch. The room is used for the Order's June "business" meeting. The Queen, as sovereign of the Order, sits in a throne at the end of the room, while the knights conduct their ceremonial conclave.

Next is the most French of the state apartments, the Grand Reception Room. In front of the window at the narrow end of the room, which overlooks the North Terrace and Eton College beyond, stands an enormous green malachite vase. The gift of Czar Nicholas I to Queen Victoria, the giant urn is really concrete covered with a thin layer of malachite, the top rim of which is badly chipped. One wonders how on earth this huge object of ceremonial magnificence could have gotten so banged up.

What had been the original banqueting room in Edward III's castle, St. George's Hall, has been transformed into a room twice as big, the largest at Windsor. The most notable feature is the imposing ceiling covered with the many-colored shields of more than 900 Garter knights, a truly impressive sight.

The Queen's Guard Chamber is another room whose walls are decorated with weapons. The first of the smaller and more personal of the state apartments shown on the visitor's tour, it leads into the Queen's Presence Chamber and then the Queen's Audience Chamber, the Queen's Ballroom and the Queen's Drawing Room. This range of rooms was the preserve of Catherine of Braganza, consort to Charles II. The Queen's Ballroom was known for many years as the Van Dyck Room, but many of the paintings by this great court artist are now in the Queen's Drawing Room. The latter became the first room of a series on this north side of the state apartments which George IV used as accommodations for State visitors after he had the royal family's suite moved to another wing.

Following it are the King's Closet (originally Charles II's private sitting room), the King's Dressing Room, the King's State Bedchamber (in a palace notably lacking in privacy, the king's bedroom was one of the few secluded places, so Charles came to use this room somewhat along the lines of a cabinet room, eventually preferring to sleep in his dressing room), the King's Drawing Room (in which George IV's body lay in state after his death in 1830), and the King's Dining Room, the last of the state apartments.

These chambers of Charles II are in themselves miniature art galleries. In the small Dressing Room are pictures by Holbein, Dürer, Van Dyck, Steen, Vermeer, Cuyp, Rubens and Rembrandt, the State Bedchamber is full of Canalettos and Gainsboroughs, the Closet another gallery of Canalettos. The furniture is, of course, almost all of an order that is rarely seen outside great museums. Just one of the thousands of antique weapons on the walls would fetch a small fortune. Windsor is a veritable Fort Knox of art treasures. Every imaginable kind of collection is housed here— weapons, priceless books, military decorations, royal iconography, even the bullet which killed Nelson at Trafalgar, ensconced in its own exquisite little case. Everywhere the visitor turns in the castle, he is confronted with some artifact, always unique, usually almost beyond price, chronicling the long history of royal Britain.

One of the world's supreme bijoux is kept at Windsor— Queen Mary's Doll's House. This miniature house, built to a scale of one inch to one foot, is anything but a "doll's house." It represents a nobleman's residence decorated in the height of fashion during the reign of King George V. Designed by Sir Edwin Lutyens (who also designed the cenotaph in Whitehall), it was the gift of the nation to Queen Mary in 1924. The house contains absolutely perfect small things of every imaginable description: 700 paintings by leading British artists, books by the likes of Kipling and Chesterton, as well as 168 other authors, taps with running water, working elevators and electric lights, even a garage with six beautiful old cars—everything at the scale of 1:12. The whole affair is housed in its own room on the castle's North Terrace, set on a dais with stepped galleries running around it, much as the Crown Jewels are displayed in the Tower of

London. The Doll's House provides a dazzling record of pre-war British craftsmanship, and would be virtually impossible to duplicate today.

The remainder of the Upper Ward is closed to the public. Guests of the Queen are usually entertained in the private apartments in the east wing's principal floor (not to be confused with the Queen's private suite in the south wing). These supremely elegant rooms were redecorated by Queen Mary in the Regency style, and vie with even the state rooms in Buckingham Palace in their magnificence. Opening onto each other through carved Chippendale doors, they are named after their primary colors, the Crimson, Green and White Drawing Rooms. The northernmost—the Crimson—leads into the State Dining Room. Off its west side at the northeast corner of the quadrangle, and directly over the Visitor's Entrance, is the private chapel. Running along the inner perimeter of both the south and east wings' principal floor in one 500-foot-long curved sweep is the spacious Grand Corridor, which serves as a magnificent art gallery as well as giving access to the main rooms of the private apartments.

The personal suite of the royal family is at the southeast corner of the quadrangle, continuing along the south wing. The Sovereign's Entrance, the porticoed entryway used by the family, is at this same juncture. It opens onto the staff offices located on the ground floor of these wings, and rises to the Queen's suite on the principal floor. Directly over the Sovereign's Entrance is what was once the gloomy old Oak Dining Room (Queen Victoria's breakfast room) which Queen Elizabeth II has converted into a modern living room, decorated in white and gold with gold draperies and a cherry-red carpet. Under the glittering crystal chandelier is a statue of her favorite racehorse, Aureole.

On the outer walls at the southeast corner is the Queen's Tower, at one time called the Victoria Tower. The rooms in this square turret were the personal apartments of Queen Victoria, and every queen of England since has occupied them. The present queen has remodeled several of its rooms.

Continuing along the Grand Corridor in the south wing are more personal rooms of the royal family, including bedroom and sitting-room suites and the offices of the Queen and Prince Philip. The last turret to the west is the Edward III Tower. The Queen decided her own family's suite of rooms in this rounded tower could legitimately reflect the best of her reign's own style, and consequently has had them decorated by Sir Hugh and Lady Casson (Sir Hugh, president of the Royal Academy of Arts, designed the famous Mall decorations for the 1953 Coronation) in a modern, light and airy decor, considered one of the most beautiful contemporary interiors in Britain.

Finally, there is Windsor Castle's setting. Stretching to the south of the castle, and covering 2,500 acres, are the Home Park and Windsor Great Park. The smaller Home Park (700 acres) really constitutes the castle's grounds, although a small part of it can be visited by the public. Frogmore House, the home once closely associated with Queen Victoria's mother, the Duchess of Kent, stands near the Frogmore Mausoleum (open one day a year to the public), the burial place of Victoria and Albert. A burial ground for members of the royal family was laid out behind the mausoleum in 1928.

The much larger Great Park affords the Queen privacy for indulging her favorite pastime of riding—part of the park is closed to all but the royal family and its guests. The Queen Mother's home, The Royal Lodge, is in the middle of the park just beyond the end of the Long Walk. At the south edge is Fort Belvedere (built in 1750, but converted by Wyatville into a country retreat in 1827), the private home of the Duke of Windsor when he was Prince of Wales and King.

SANDRINGHAM

Of the Queen's four principal residences, Sandringham and Balmoral are, unlike Buckingham Palace and Windsor Castle, her private property. Both are always bequeathed to the sovereign's heir, thus being settled on the new monarch with the death of the old, and by virtue of the monarch's exemption from death duties, avoiding any diminution by taxation. When Edward VIII abdicated in 1936, the new King George VI had to buy the properties from his elder brother. Informed sources put the amount he paid for the two estates at £1,000,000 plus £60,000 annually for life. Their combined value today is at least 10 times what it was in 1936.

The setting of the Sandringham estate—20,000 acres on the flat windswept coastal edge of Norfolk and about 110 miles northeast of London—is not one of England's more attractive, the weather combining with the terrain to make it fairly forbidding. But ever since Edward VII, as Prince of Wales, and Alexandra made it their country home shortly after being married, it has been a much-beloved retreat by nearly every sovereign, Edward VIII the unsurprising exception.

What had been an unprepossessing estate of the Prime Minister Lord Palmerston's stepson, Charles Cowper, was selected by the Prince Consort with characteristic briskness to serve as the country home for his eldest son. Albert died before the deal was closed; wishing to adhere to the decision of his dead father, the Prince of Wales bought the property in the summer of 1862. He paid Cowper £220,000—a fabulous sum at the time—for the house and acreage (then 7,000 acres, the remaining 13,000 acres having been purchased by succeeding monarchs).

The original early 19th-century house was soon torn down and rebuilt in a neo-Elizabethan style then popular for the country homes of England's landed aristocracy; the rebuilding cost £80,000. The new Sandringham was built during an unfortunate period for British architecture, and the rambling brick mansion with its multi-gabled facade had nothing especially majestic about it. It looked like the mansion of any successful brewer. But the prince and his new princess loved it, not the least for its modernity, including newfangled plumbing, the installation of which had been personally supervised by Thomas Crapper, the inventor of the modern toilet whose name eventually became a household word.

Throughout their long marriage, Edward and Alexandra felt totally at home when at Sandringham, a sentiment shared exactly by their son and grandson, George V and George VI. Both kings died in the mansion, 16 years apart. Edward VIII spent one day at Sandringham as King. Although not so intimately bound to the estate by childhood ties, Elizabeth II has come to have a warm regard for the drafty house, which at somewhere between 600 and 700 rooms and with a facade 450 feet long is the largest still-private house in Britain.

Instead of entering a grand reception hall, the main door opens directly into the Great Saloon. (Rooms in royal residences *always* have proper names.) There is today a folding Oriental screen at an angle to the door to give something of the effect of an entry hall, but the overall impression is still startlingly different from that of the other royal homes. The Ballroom, Library and many other rooms have been added piecemeal over the years. The most beautiful room in the house is the white, gold and blue Main Drawing Room, reflecting the elegance of Queen Alexandra's taste—a room still hauntingly reminiscent of the silken splendors of Edwardian high society. The house is literally crammed with souvenirs of its successive owners, from inconsequential bibelots to the almost priceless collection of Fabergé objets so beloved of Queen Alexandra, a taste probably picked up from her sister, the Dowager Empress of Russia.

For decades, Sandringham was the house where the royal family spent Christmas. The present Queen and her family have recently changed that tradition, now gathering at Windsor with most of the cousins—Kents, Gloucesters—as well as Princess Margaret and her children and the Queen Mother. But on December 26—Boxing Day—the whole group still packs up and heads for Sandringham for New Year's. Besides, the Queen likes to be as close as possible to the two racehorse studs she runs on the estate.

Plans were made in 1974 to modernize the house, involving the demolition of 91 rooms. The Queen at first decided against the improvements, feeling it would be a public relations mistake to spend the estimated £400,000 when so many of her subjects were barely getting by in Britain's semi-permanent recession. But the following year, she went ahead with the demolition and rebuilding anyway.

Since 1977, five of the principal ground-floor rooms—the Saloon, the Main Drawing Room, the Smaller Drawing Room, the Long Corridor and the Dining Room—have been open to the public in the summer months.

York Cottage, the pokey little house that was home to King George V and Queen Mary from the time of their wedding until Queen Alexandra's death in 1925, is on the Sandringham estate. The Victorian Gothic villa was probably the smallest of Britain's royal residences, but their six children grew up in the house in which all but the oldest (the late Duke of Windsor) were born. Since Edward VII stipulated in his will that his widow should live in the main house after his death, George and Mary weren't able to move into it until 15 years after coming to the throne. The incongruity of staying in the big house while the King and Queen and their considerable brood overfilled York Cottage never seemed to occur to Alexandra. (Apparently no thought was given to sharing the 600-odd rooms.) Moving out of York Cottage and into the main house after 33 years must have been a genuine pleasure for the shamelessly acquisitive Queen Mary. York Cottage is no longer used as a royal residence, but today houses Sandringham estate offices on the first floor and apartments for estate officials on the second floor.

One other house on the estate is Appleton, which was once the country home of King George V's sister, Queen Maud of Norway. It has not been occupied since her death in 1938 except for short periods during the War when the specially bomb-proofed building housed Princesses Elizabeth and Margaret on visits to the Sandringham estate.

BALMORAL

If suddenly the royal family had to undergo an austerity program and somehow manage with only one of their private residences, their sentimental favorite would undoubtedly be Balmoral. It is Balmoral, the monarch's summer home, where royal hearts beat happiest.

One hundred miles north of Edinburgh, overlooking the River Dee in the Scottish highlands, the imposing fairy-tale castle squats stolidly, adorned with turrets and keep and surrounded by stunningly beautiful grounds. Every August, the Queen and the Duke of Edinburgh travel north in their private railway carriage to spend a two-month Deeside holiday.

Just as she likes to be thought of as squire at Sandringham, so at Balmoral Elizabeth II prefers the role of laird—roughly "Lord of the Manor." Balmoral is the last ves-

tige of total privacy for the royal family now that Sandringham House has been opened to the public. Although
the grounds (or "policies," as the Scots call them) of Balmoral
are shown to visiting tourists when the Queen is not in residence, no part of the house itself is ever opened to the public.

Since medieval times a fortified manor has stood on the
site. The original medieval estate was called "Bouchmorale,"
Gaelic for "majestic dwelling," but the beginnings of the
present royal residence came when Victoria and Albert fell
in love with the Aberdeenshire retreat and bought it for
£31,000 in 1852. Much of the rebuilding was carried out
with £250,000 bequeathed at the time to the Queen by
an eccentric Scottish miner named Neald. She deduced in
her diary that he did it because he knew she "would not
waste it." Victoria and her husband became so caught up
with their Scottish home that some wags referred to their
stiff court behavior as "Balmorality."

The rebuilding of the existing house came about because Albert wanted to have a reminder of his native Thurin-
gia in Germany. A mock-Gothic castle was built much
resembling his ancestral Coburg home, Rosenau. The craftsmanship was superb, the very best of the era. The castle is
adorned with exceptionally fine examples of mid-Victorian
taste; it suffers less from gloomy "tartanitis" than is popu-
larly imagined.

The dominating feature is a square 80-foot-high tower,
surmounted by a 20-foot turret from which the Royal Standard flies when the Queen is in residence. From the porte
cochere, the hall opens to the main corridor running along
the center of the building. This entry area, with its life-sized
marble statue of the Prince Consort which now sometimes
gets used as a hat rack, is the only ponderous section of the
house, the remainder being opened with broad, high windows. The Grand Staircase rises from the center of the hall,
leading to the private royal apartments on the second floor.

The Ballroom is, at 25 feet by 68 feet, the largest in the residence; the Ghillies (gamekeepers) Balls, at which the Queen and Prince Philip entertain their staff, are held here.

The Dining Room, Drawing Room, Billiard Room and Library are on the first floor. The whole building will house about 100 people, but only rarely does the Queen have very large parties of weekend guests. (Since this is her private home, no Court Circular listing the guests is printed.)

The entire estate covers about 24,000 acres, on which there are also two other royal homes. Birkhall, a relatively small old-fashioned three-storey house, is the residence of the Queen Mother when she is visiting her family on their Balmoral holiday. Abergeldie Castle, now closed, was the Scottish home of Edward VII as Prince of Wales. It had once been the home of his grandmother, the Duchess of Kent. It was last used by the Gloucesters and Kents during family gatherings at Balmoral.

OTHER ROYAL HOMES

The Queen Mother has three primary residences: Clarence House in London, The Royal Lodge in Windsor Great Park and the Castle of Mey in Scotland. Clarence House, located just down the Mall from Buckingham Palace, next door to St. James's Palace, was designed by Nash in 1825 for William IV when he was still Duke of Clarence. He and Queen Adelaide lived in it during his seven-year reign (the only sovereign to do so during his actual reign). He hated the still-unfinished Buckingham Palace, considering it "sepulchral," and encouraged its delay in completion. After his death, his widow continued to occupy the mansion alone, followed by the brief occupancy of Princess Augusta, the sixth child of George III, and Queen Victoria's aunt. Next came Victoria's mother, the Duchess of Kent, in turn succeeded by her second son, the Duke of Edinburgh, who was there from 1866 to 1900. (During this period, his brother, the Prince of Wales, was practically next door at Marlborough House.) From the Duke of Edinburgh's death in 1900 until his own in 1942, the Duke of Connaught, Queen Victoria's third son, lived in Clarence House.

It looked very much different in the Edinburgh and Connaught days, darkened with a forest of antlers and other ponderous paraphernalia fashionable in the late Victorian era. Great ugly gasoliers hung in place of today's delicate crystal chandeliers and suits of medieval armor clashed with Nash's lovely boiserie. Not a single bathroom existed in the entire mansion.

The one time the palatial residence has served as other than a royal home was from 1942 until 1947, when it became, at the King's suggestion, headquarters of the British Red Cross and the St. John Ambulance Brigade. In 1947, it became the townhouse of Princess Elizabeth and the Duke of Edinburgh, its second occupancy by a Duke of Edinburgh. It was completely restored to its original Georgian elegance for them, with the addition of modern heating and plumbing. Princess Anne was born there in 1950. (Prince Charles was born in Buckingham Palace.) On the Queen's accession in 1952, Clarence House became the Queen Mother's London residence.

The best word to describe the house is "elegant." A classical marble portico opens into a coolly beautiful entrance corridor where stairs lead up to a spacious cream-colored double drawing room, divided by paired Corinthian columns into two squares, carpeted with pale Aubusson rugs, and lighted by huge Waterford-style crystal chandeliers. It's a perfect reflection of the Queen Mother's taste—silky and sumptuous.

At Clarence House, the Queen Mother breakfasts each morning to the (some would say) bizarre sound of a piper playing in the garden. This little extravagance is traditional in the royal family; her elder daughter enjoys the same luxury. The pipers come courtesy of the British Army.

The visitor having an appointment with a member of the Queen Mother's Household enters the royal precinct through the Ambassador's Court portal. The Household offices, technically a part of St. James's Palace rather than Clarence House (these offices were occupied by the Lord Chamberlain's staff until the 1930s), are attached to the residence through a completely integrated set of corridors and archways; the arrangement leaves the Queen Mother's house itself officially free of any mundane workaday incursions. On arriving at Clarence Gate, the short street leading into Ambassador's Court, the visitor is stopped by a pair of policemen at a barricade, another ubiquitous reminder of the continuous and random acts of terrorism plaguing the United Kingdom. The Household official who has made your appointment has given the policeman your name; after the list is checked to see if you're on it, you are escorted to the Household entrance, a beautiful glossy black door with a brass knocker polished to a mirrorlike gleam, where you are left on your own to ring the bell. A butler answers and shows the visitor into a sitting room, the kind of room which the inherited rich take for granted: all terribly comfortable and chintzy, with silver-framed photographs of the Queen Mother on mantels and end tables. As at Buckingham Palace, the butler hands you the *Telegraph* (presumably together with the *Times* when the latter isn't on strike), and with the courtesy peculiar to royal venues, leaves to notify whichever official it is you're there to see.

Captain Alastair Aird, CVO (Commander Victorian Order), Comptroller and Extra Equerry to the Queen Mother, is, after the Queen Mother's Lord Chamberlain (a mostly honorary position now held by Major the Earl of Dalhousie), the ranking official at Clarence House. A member of

Queen Elizabeth's staff for 20 years, Aird still considers himself the "new boy"; turnover is not a problem in the higher echelons of the Queen Mother's service. Born in 1931, he was educated at Eton and became a captain in the Queen's 9th Lancers. He is a cousin of Sir John Aird, Bart., equerry to the last three sovereigns. The position he holds, equivalent to Master of the Household at Buckingham Palace, entails running an organization tiny compared to that of the Queen, but very much larger than that of any other member of the royal family.

Captain Aird is the quintessential courtier—polished, urbane and handsome. His office is a retreat from the depressing urban realities of modern London just outside the privileged walls he works within. The impression the visitor receives is that he is running "The Queen Mother, Ltd." In a way, royals *are* treated as a kind of highly up-market commercial firm—at Clarence House, Aird is the manager and the Queen Mother is the product. Discussing her activities and schedule, one tends to lose sight of the fact that the object of the conversation is an 80-year-old widowed great-grandmother. In this case, it's rather like thinking of this lovely and gracious lady as a commodity, apportioned out to a reverent but demanding public.

Next in command at Clarence House is Lieutenant Colonel Sir Martin Gilliat, KCVO (Knight Commander Victorian Order), MBE (Member [of the Order of the] British Empire), and who like Aird has a "grace and favor" flat in St. James's Palace; their front doors, marked with brass plaques, are just off the sidewalk at the Marlborough Road end of the palace. Another Eton graduate, Gilliat became Assistant Private Secretary to the Queen Mother in 1955 and Private Secretary the following year. He is an equerry as well, the position being kind of a male lady-in-waiting. The job of Private Secretary at Clarence House is very much different from the same job at Buckingham Palace in that the latter contributes significantly to royal policy formulation by the obvious virtue of nearness to the throne.

The Queen Mother's Household (the word always, by the way, spelled with a capital "H" to differentiate it from mere staff members or servants) includes a Press Officer, now Major Arthur Griffin (these former Regular Army officers on the Queen Mother's staff still use their military ranks as titles because it was the wish of King George VI that ex-officers attached to the palace after the War be so addressed; the Queen Mother, and the Queen to a lesser extent, have since maintained the tradition), Apothecary (physician), and a whole raft of ladies-in-waiting, led by the Mistress of the Robes, the Duchess of Abercorn; two Ladies of the Bedchamber, the Dowager Viscountess Hambelden and the Baroness Grimthorpe; two Extra Ladies-in-Waiting, the Dowager Baroness Harlech and the Dowager Countess of Scarborough; four Women of the Bedchamber and five Extra Women of the Bedchamber. (The ladies take turns serving on a rota basis; the one actually on duty stays at Clarence House.) The Queen Mother chooses among these Household members to lunch with her when she is not officially entertaining or having family in for lunch.

When visiting her daughter and son-in-law at Windsor on weekends, Queen Elizabeth stays at The Royal Lodge, another Nash mansion in Windsor Great Park. It was King George V who insisted that the name always be preceded by "The" with a capitalized "T." "People will know it's really royal," he snorted. An angular, three-storey building, painted pink to match the Queen Mother's taste, it stands secluded amid the trees that spread south from Windsor Castle. The Royal Lodge was King George VI's favorite retreat for relaxation, and it was where he went to recuperate after his leg and lung operations. It is still much beloved by the Queen Mother.

Queen Elizabeth's very own retreat from the spotlight (which she never really wants to get *too* far away from) is an old Scottish mansion, the Castle of Mey. Overlooking Pentland Firth near John o' Groat's at the northernmost tip of Scotland, the castle is a rambling affair and looks like something out of the Brothers Grimm. The Queen Mother bought the 16th-century wreck in her early widowhood, and by 1955 had it completely restored. She now visits it two or three times a year. Each summer, the Queen and Duke of Edinburgh round the tip of Britain on the royal yacht *Britannia*, and the small liner's whistle blows a long salute to their favorite lady.

Until recently, the official country residence of the Prince of Wales was Chevening (rhymes with evening) House, near Chipstead, in Kent. Charles rarely visited the place—it is 22 miles southeast, the wrong direction, socially speaking, from London. (West—toward Windsor—is the *proper* polo and fox-hunting direction.)

The house was designed by Inigo Jones, the great 17th-century architect, and with its 3,500 acres and endowment of over £1,000,000, was bequeathed to the nation by the Earl Stanhope on his death in 1967. It was his intention that it become the official seat of a ranking member of the royal family, or failing that, a cabinet minister. In May 1974, Prince Charles decided he wanted to take the estate, and got his mother's permission to do so, following which extensive renovations and redecoration were carried out.

In June 1980, Charles officially gave up his tenancy of Chevening, the public excuse being that his many commitments prevented his getting to maintain and use it very often. Within a few weeks, the palace revealed that the Duchy of Cornwall had bought a nine-bedroom, 18th-century mansion deep in the heart of rural England's Gloucestershire, and in which the Prince of Wales will be the "tenant." The estimated sale price was $2,370,000. The Georgian mansion, called High Grove, is at 30 main rooms a good deal smaller than Chevening. Notwithstanding his new 347-acre estate, Charles's main residence, at least until after his marriage, will probably continue to be his comfortable and richly furnished suite of rooms on the bedroom floor of Buckingham Palace's east wing. It is thought that the most likely eventual home for the Prince and Princess of Wales while awaiting accession to the throne will be Clarence House.

There was something of an uproar when the Queen spent an estimated £725,000 on Gatcombe Park for her daughter and son-in-law. Not an unusual thing for an extremely rich woman to do, except that Britons supposedly were being asked to tighten their belts and their Queen was spending more than most of them would ever lay their hands on for the unpopular Princess. The Gloucestershire mansion with its 750 acres had belonged to R. A. "Rab" Butler, the former Tory politician who had just missed becoming Prime Minister in the fifties. The acreage, two-thirds of which is prime farmland, lies 20 miles from Anne's in-laws in Wiltshire. The Princess and her husband are continuing to run the estate as a farming enterprise with a beef breeding herd of 190 head of cattle, as well as wheat and barley crops.

Gatcombe Park is a graystone mansion in the Georgian style, with a classical square portico flanked by two bayed conservatory-like rooms. Sweeping lawns, a huge greenhouse, white shutters, roses, jasmine and wisteria climbing the walls, and that fancy heated footbath for the horses—all the elements for a proper setting for a princess, even a slightly pugnacious one.

The London home of Princess Margaret is a flat in Kensington Palace, Wren's lovely brick mansion at the west end of Kensington Gardens, smack in the center of town. The grace and favor apartment, Number 1A, is nothing overly grand, but then neither is it the sort of thing your ordinary middle-manager comes home to. The main problem Margaret has is the hordes of tourists swarming through the state rooms of the palace and the gardens, although they are very carefully kept from getting too near to 1A.

The Princess's holiday home is half a world away. On her 1960 wedding, her old and close friend Colin Tennant offered her a chunk of his Caribbean island of Mustique as a wedding present. ("Would you like a bit of my island? Or something I can wrap up and send to you?") Ten years later, Margaret asked her husband's uncle, designer Oliver Messel, to come up with plans for a house on the isolated three-mile-long island. The result was a small, beautiful neo-Georgian vacation cottage with an open and sunny living room flanked on either side by two-bedroom wings, the whole embracing a flagstone courtyard. The home is enchanting, looking off over an island-dotted blue sea, completely private (although her cousin Lord Lichfield has bought a neighboring property) and quietly luxurious. The only picture in the house is a photograph of the Annigoni portrait of the Queen in her Garter robes, something the Princess says is there "to show it's an English home." The furniture is covered in chintz, the virtual signature fabric of the royal family. The Mustique house is the only home Margaret actually owns.

Other peripheral members of the royal family have grace and favor flats. Princess Alexandra has a pied-à-terre in St. James's Palace's Friary Court; her main home is another grace and favor residence in Hyde Park. (The latter replaced Thatched House Lodge in Richmond Park, a "modest" house of six reception rooms, four bathrooms, a heated pool, stables and four acres of gardens, but which was plagued by jets flying directly overhead.) The Duke and Duchess of

Gloucester have a 35-room flat in Kensington Palace and are Princess Margaret's neighbors; an adjacent apartment, until recently occupied by Princess Alice, Countess of Athlone, who died in January 1981, is called Clock House. The Duke and Duchess of Kent have an apartment in St. James's Palace, next door to Clarence House, as well as a grace and favor house in Norfolk, Anmer Hall. Prince and Princess Michael of Kent also have a flat in St. James's Palace.

Many of the country homes associated with the British royal family since Queen Victoria's time are now either government offices or in private hands. Fort Belvedere, King Edward VIII's retreat, which was last occupied by the Queen's cousins, the Gerald Lascelles, for a time in the fifties, was recently bought by the Sultan of Dubai. (Barnwell Manor, the 40-room country home of the Gloucesters in Northamptonshire, 80 miles from London, is still the country home of the new Duke and Duchess, as well as Princess Alice of Gloucester.) Upkeep on these places is ruinous. Marlborough House, the palace on the Mall which was the home of Edward VII and Alexandra before their accession and of Queen Mary in her widowhood, is now a Commonwealth meeting center. In addition to holding 20 grace and favor flats, St. James's Palace is used for a great variety of purposes, such as the Chancery for the orders of knighthood and for the Marshal of the Diplomatic Corps.

One remaining royal residence, still in use although on a very limited basis, is Holyroodhouse in Edinburgh. It is the Queen's official Scottish residence. Forever associated with Queen Mary of Scotland, the room in which Rizzio was murdered in 1567 is on public view. The state apartments have French and Flemish tapestries and 18th-century furniture which is particularly linked with Victoria and Albert, who often stayed there. Altogether, it's a fairly gloomy pile, and the Queen probably doesn't look forward to the few days she spends there on her annual official visits to Scotland's capital.

A word about "grace and favor" residences. There are 121 of these dwellings, located mostly at Hampton Court Palace (whose last resident King was George II), Kensington Palace, Windsor Castle, Buckingham Palace and St. James's Palace. Hampton Court has 27 such flats, Kensington Palace has 13, including the one for Princess Margaret. These are all bestowed entirely at the discretion of the Queen to members of her family as well as to family retainers, many of whom are retired. They are rent-free to the tenants, but any repairs or alterations are at the occupants' expense. The 20 apartments in St. James's Palace range from a two-room flat to the section known as York House, the London residence of the Duke of Windsor when he was Prince of Wales and for most of his tenure as King. Prince William of Gloucester had a flat in the palace consisting of a bedroom, bathroom and sitting room. One apartment for many years belonged to Amos, the butler left behind by the departing ex-King in 1936. Most of the palace's apartments are now occupied by the great officers of State or members of the Household. There are also a few grace and favor residences sprinkled throughout the rest of the country.

One of the official Jubilee portraits of the Queen, shown wearing the circlet tiara and the Jubilee Necklace, as well as the Family Orders of her father and grandfather. *Photo Peter Grugeon, Camera Press London*

Family portrait commemorating the Queen Mother's eightieth birthday. *Front row, left to right:* Princess Margaret, the Queen, the Queen Mother, Princess Anne. *Back row, left to right:* Viscount Linley, Lady Sarah Armstrong-Jones, Prince Andrew, the Duke of Edinburgh, the Prince of Wales, Prince Edward, Captain Mark Phillips. *Camera Press (The Times) London*

The White Drawing Room in Buckingham Palace. *Central Press Photos*

The unseen garden, or west, facade of Buckingham Palace. The ground-floor room in the center is the Bow Room; directly above is the Music Room. *Central Press Photos*

The new Princess of Wales, formerly Lady Diana Spencer, seen shortly before her engagement outside her flat. *U.P.I. Photo*

The Throne Dais in Buckingham Palace's Throne Room, photographed during the reign of King George VI. *Central Press Photos*

Aerial view of Windsor Castle, with the city of Windsor in the foreground. *Camera Press* (Photoflight) *London*

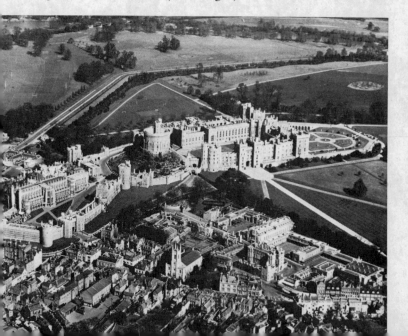

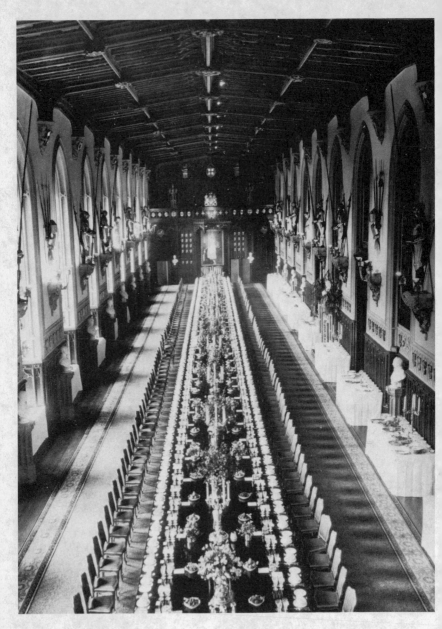

St. George's Hall, Windsor Castle, seen from the throne end of the room.
Central Press Photos

Sandringham House, seen from the garden, or west, front. *Photo E. E. Swain Ltd., copyright Her Majesty the Queen*

Balmoral Castle in the '20s. *Central Press Photos*

Clarence House, the London home of the Queen Mother. The Ambassador's Court entrance is around the rear of the house—to the left in this photo. *Central Press Photos*

The Royal Lodge—the five ground-floor windows enclose the Saloon. *Hamlyn Group Picture Library*

Gatcombe Park, home of Princess Anne and Captain Mark Phillips. *Photo Richard Slade, Camera Press London*

Michael Shea, Press Secretary to the Queen, seen at Buckingham Palace's forecourt gate. The Privy Purse Door is over his left shoulder. *Central Press Photos*

St. Edward's Crown—*the Crown of England. Central Press Photos, Crown copyright reserved*

The Coronation Crown of Queen Elizabeth (the present Queen Mother). So far used only once, it may one day be worn by the Queen Consort of Charles at their coronation. *Central Press Photos*

Cecil Beaton's famous photo of the Queen taken after her coronation. *U.P.I. (U.K.) Photo*

3

Court
THE QUEEN, LTD.

"The Court" is one of those terms which everybody seems to vaguely understand, but which few can really pin down. The very concept of a court is so archaic to most people today as to be something almost exclusively associated with history books. But the Court of St. James's—that is, the British court—is very much alive, functioning as smoothly as a Rolls-Royce limousine. The royal establishment has its headquarters at Buckingham Palace, but it is spread over the entire kingdom, from the Lord Chamberlain's office in St. James's Palace to the estates of the various members of the royal family, from the Royal Air Force command center of the Queen's Flight to the Royal Company of Archers, Archers Hall, Edinburgh. It all forms a sort of "Department of the Crown," a neat package which doesn't exist in reality, but which not a few members of Parliament wish did, so as to more easily administer the Crown.

The Court can best be thought of today as the body of bureaucrats who make the monarchy "go." Some of these people are ensconced in the folds of high and mighty titles of ancient origin, and only occasionally serve the Crown. Others are full-time workers little distinguishable from their thousands of fellow workers who man the high-rises of commerce all over Britain. The most logical place to begin describing the British Court is at its center—Buckingham Palace.

Running the palace is akin to running a large hotel. There are 337 full-time and 126 part-time employees, who receive an aggregate salary of more than £1,000,000 annually. These employees are divided into three rigidly distinct castes: Household, Officials and Clerks, and Staff. The members of the first group can without equivocation be classified as "courtiers"; the members of the second group can marginally be included within the definition of "the court," but they aren't really "courtiers"; and the third group—the servants, cleaners, and so forth—doesn't count, socially speaking.

Those at the top of the pecking order, the Household, are essentially the ones who come into direct contact with the Queen on a routine basis. Most Household members have under them Officials and Clerks, who in turn have Staff reporting to them. It all pretty much adds up to a typical organization chart. A common thread running through the Household is that most of its members were former military or naval officers. A senior member of the Queen Mother's Household commented that the discipline and training of the Services is found to be uncommonly useful in royal employment.

Officially, the senior members of the Household are, in order, the Lord Chamberlain (currently Lord Maclean), the Lord Steward (the Duke of Northumberland), and the Master of the Horse (the Earl of Westmorland), responsible respectively for "above stairs," "below stairs" and "out of doors." In reality, the senior royal servant is the Queen's Private Secretary, now Sir Philip Moore.

The Lord Chamberlain was originally a deputy of the Lord Great Chamberlain (see page 98 under Great Officers of State), but he is now independent of his nominal superior, and is the highest-ranking member of the Court. Lord Maclean lives in a grace and favor residence in St. James's Palace and at his ancestral home, Duart Castle in Scotland.

The duties of the Lord Chamberlain, whose job is not a full-time one, include responsibility for the direction of all State and Court ceremonies—except coronations and funerals, which are under the Earl Marshal—and, symbolically, he is the Queen's emissary to the House of Lords. Lord Maclean, the holder of a life barony created in 1971 and the 27th chief of the Clan Maclean, is responsible for the organization of the many State visits to Britain of foreign heads of state. He appoints the majority of Household members, a large number of whom serve part-time as he does. Under him is a great list of officials with impressive-sounding titles: Lords-in-Waiting, the Comptroller of the Lord Chamberlain's Office, Gentlemen Ushers, the Keeper of the Swans, and the Poet Laureate, to name a few.

There are nine Lords-in-Waiting, including two permanent Lords, the Lord Cobbold, who held the office of Lord Chamberlain before Lord Maclean, and the Lord Charteris of Amisfield. All of the two dozen or so Gentlemen Ushers and Extra Gentlemen Ushers—mostly high-ranking retired Army and Navy officers—serve the Queen at large functions such as garden parties and investitures. As with all of these titular offices, the honor of holding them far outweighs the rigors of any of the duties associated with them.

The Lord Steward's bailiwick covers the complex domestic management of the palace, the cooks and maids, butlers and footmen. In practice, however, the duties of the mostly ceremonial Lord Steward are carried out by the Master of the Household, a full-time position held by Vice-Admiral Sir Peter Ashmore. For example, catering arrangements are under Sir Peter. Food service constitutes a matter of some intricacy in the giant palace. Not only does the kitchen have to meet the needs of the royal family, but it cooks for the huge State banquets to which hundreds of guests are invited. Fortunately, it no longer has to worry about making carloads of cookies for the three annual Garden Parties; the palace hires an outside catering firm for these functions.

Sir Peter, who was Chief of Allied Staff at NATO Naval Headquarters before his current appointment, has control over a sundry mix of palace departments and functions, including the Court Post Office and the palace police. The mail from all the royal establishments in London—Clarence House, St. James's Palace and Kensington Palace—is brought to the Buckingham Palace post office to be mailed, without stamps, the royal frank being all that's necessary for the Queen to send her and her family's and her Household's mail through the British postal system.

Sir Peter's jurisdiction also includes the Court Circular, that marvelously anachronistic little record of the royal family's official movements and engagements which the *Telegraph* (the London daily allied officially to the Conservative Party) publishes daily. The Circular never loses its tone of detached coolness. Reading the Court column for the period during the height of the Blitz, December 1940 (in the *Times*, which still carries it), provides a lesson in the immutability of the British Crown. The daily chronicling of lords- and ladies-in-waiting being regularly rotated, audiences being granted to rural vicars on retirement, ambassadors being received—all went on as if the city around the palace weren't being pounded into rubble. Today, the Press Secretary's office considers itself fortunate that the Master of the Household, and not itself, gets to worry about this particular bit of royal miscellany.

The Master of the Horse, a title which of course originated in the pre-automobile era, is responsibile not only for the royal stables which hold the world's most splendid carriages and coaches and some of its most pampered horses, but also for the automobiles—mostly Rolls-Royces—which

the Queen and her family use. As Master of the Horse, the
duties of Lord Westmorland (who succeeded the Duke of
Beaufort, a close friend of the Queen, in 1978) are mostly
symbolic and ceremonial, although in the past this office was
a politically powerful one. The day-to-day job of running the
Royal Mews is carried out by Lord Westmorland's deputy,
titled the Crown Equerry, Lieutenant Colonel Sir John Man-
sell Miller, another Eton-Guards-polo-playing member of
Britain's top crust. The 20 or so cars of which he is in charge
include a £60,000 Phantom Six Rolls-Royce given to the
Queen in 1978 as a Jubilee gift. The mostly maroon-colored
fleet contains cars fitted with large glass areas and raised rear
seats so as to allow the public a good view of the monarch.
The Rolls-Royces have replaced the Daimlers of the Queen's
grandfather's day; they have no license plates, displaying instead the royal arms on a lighted stanchion on the roof. (For
private use on her estates, the Queen drives herself in a 3.5-
liter Rover sedan.) The most magnificent vehicle in Sir
John's keeping is the State Coach, a gilded behemoth with
no equal in the world, which has been used only twice in
this reign—at the Coronation and on the drive to St. Paul's
on Silver Jubilee Day.

One of the largest departments, albeit almost entirely
ceremonial, is the Ecclesiastical Household. Headed by a
bishop who has the title "Clerk of the Closet," it includes 34
Chaplains to the Queen and three Extra Chaplains to the
Queen, all of whom theoretically see to Her Majesty's spiritual refreshment. The various Chapels Royal—Windsor,
Sandringham, and so forth—are under the control of this
branch. The Queen's chaplains are assigned to conduct services and preach on a rota basis. The chaplain on duty does
have the assurance that he will almost always have the
Queen's ear at these services. Elizabeth II attends regular
Sunday services, taking her role as Defender of the Church
of England seriously. The Clerk of the Closet himself in ear-

lier days had the duty "to attend at the right hand of the Sovereign in the Royal Closet during Divine Service to resolve such doubts as may arise concerning spiritual matters"; the post is today for the most part honorific.

The Medical Household is under the "Head of the Medical Household and Physician," Sir Richard Bayliss, M.D. Reporting to him is a whole battery of medical specialists who help ensure the Queen's good health—sergeant-surgeons, surgeon-oculists, apothecary to the Queen, and even a coroner to the Queen's Household.

The Ascot Office, housed in St. James's Palace, takes care of the arrangements surrounding the royal family's annual pilgrimage to Ascot. Even more important, it decides who gets into the Royal Enclosure and the Queen's Lawn, the bastions of manufactured class consciousness presided over by the leading elements of Britain's dwindling landed aristocracy. The head of the Ascot Office, titled "Her Majesty's Representative at Ascot," is the Marquess of Abergavenny.

By far the most important departments of the Household today are the Private Secretary's Office and the Department of the Keeper of the Privy Purse and Treasurer to the Queen. About halfway down the ground-floor corridor in Buckingham Palace's north wing—the Privy Purse Corridor—is an octagonally shaped junction. At the four opposing corners are painted portraits of the Queen's last four Private Secretaries, the Right Honorable Sir Alan Lascelles, Lord Adeane of Stamfordham, Lord Charteris of Amisfield (the last two, Michael Adeane and Martin Charteris, were ennobled for their services with life baronies), and the current holder of the office, the Right Honorable Sir Philip Moore, KCVO.

Lascelles served the Queen only for the first year of her reign, being replaced in 1953 by the then Lieutenant Colonel Adeane, a grandson of the Lord Stamfordham who had been

Private Secretary to both Queen Victoria and King George V. Adeane was succeeded in 1972 by his deputy of nearly 20 years, then Sir Martin Charteris. Men of remarkably similar backgrounds, both Adeane and Charteris are from noble families (Charteris is the son of Lord Elcho and grandson of the Earl of Wemyss), both were at Eton and both rose to colonelcies during World War II. Charteris, who follows his name with GCB (Grand Cross of the Order of Bath), GCVO (Grand Cross of the Victorian Order), and OBE (Officer of the Order of the British Empire), is the only British subject who can also use the initials QSO—the Queen's Service Order of New Zealand, a "perk" he obtained as Private Secretary to the Queen of New Zealand, another of his employer's titles. He is now a permanent Lord-in-Waiting and lives at the Provost's Lodge at Eton College.

In 1977, Sir Philip Moore broke this ingrown mold. The son of an Indian civil servant, he was born in 1921 and graduated from Oxford before his World War II service. That was followed by a decade in the Indian Civil Service and stints as British Deputy High Commissioner in Singapore and Chief of Public Relations at the Defense Ministry. He joined the royal Household in 1966 as Assistant Private Secretary, being promoted to Deputy Private Secretary in 1972.

The position of Private Secretary is not a particularly old one in comparison to most of the royal offices. The first incumbent was Herbert Taylor, appointed in 1805 because King George III's eyesight was failing and he needed a confidential secretary to help him carry out his chores. By the end of the century, it had grown into an immensely influential post under Queen Victoria and early in the 20th century under King Edward VII. Then the private secretaries guided the monarchs through thickets of constitutional intricacies and issues over which the sovereign's deeds and wishes still held a measure of importance. As the Queen's role in

political and legislative life is today almost totally circum-
scribed, the office of Private Secretary has correspondingly
diminished in national significance. But for matters involving
the royal house, it is this servant who is the Queen's principal adviser. The extent to which the Queen becomes involved in even slightly controversial public issues is heavily
influenced by Sir Philip.

Helped by a Deputy Private Secretary (William F. P.
Heseltine, formerly the Queen's Press Secretary) and an Assistant Private Secretary (Robert Fellowes, the husband of
Lady Jane Spencer, the daughter of Lord Spencer and sister
of Prince Charles's fiancée, Lady Diana Spencer), Moore's
office deals with all correspondence between the Queen and
her ministers, whether British or Commonwealth. Whenever
the Queen gives a speech, it is a safe bet that it was written
by her Private Secretary. (Except *the* Speech formally opening Parliament each year, composed by the Prime Minister's
office.)

Under Moore is the office of Press Secretary to the
Queen, a position first established in 1947, but directly descended from the Court Newsman, who was paid £45 a year,
appointed by George III to correct the lies everyone was telling about him.

In order to succeed as the Queen's liaison between the
palace and the press, the Press Secretary has to understand
the anachronistic nature of late-20th-century monarchy. The
Press Secretary's office is careful to stress that its function
never involves "public relations." The current secretary, Mr.
Michael Shea, is a former Deputy Director of British Infor-
mation Services in New York. He succeeded Ronald Allison,
a one-time BBC sports reporter. His two Assistant Press Secretaries are John Dauth, an Australian, and Mrs. Anne Wall,
a 51-year-old admiral's daughter and niece of Princess Alice
of Gloucester; in 1975 she married Michael Wall, Assistant
Keeper of the Privy Purse.

The second of the two offices critical to the smooth running of the monarchy is the Privy Purse Department, the Keeper also holding the title of Treasurer to the Queen. The current incumbent in these offices is Major Sir Rennie Maudslay, a former Harrow boy and officer in the King's Royal Rifle Corps. He and his assistants manage the Queen's financial affairs, including her personal financial dealings with her bankers, Messrs. Coutts and Company (now a part of Britain's largest bank, National Westminster, but allowed to retain their identity because of the inestimable cachet associated with their well-known royal connection). The agents of the Queen's various farming enterprises at Sandringham, Balmoral and Windsor are under Maudslay's direction.

Also close to the Queen are her ladies-in-waiting, all of whom are her personal choices nowadays, as opposed to the political choices of the past. They are officially called either "Ladies of the Bedchamber," usually the wives of earls, or "Women of the Bedchamber," lower ranking and often untitled (but extremely well-connected) friends of the Queen. The "ladies" attend formal events with the Queen, taking care of her umbrellas and gloves and so forth, their reward being the great honor inherent in the appointment. They are currently the Marchioness of Abergavenny and the Countess of Airlie.

The "women" accompany the Queen on less formal appointments, answer the majority of her correspondence, and perform other personal tasks. They attend the Queen on a two-week rotation basis, going everywhere with her, including her private homes in Scotland and Norfolk. The positions are now held by the Honorable Mary Morrison, Lady Susan Hussey, Lady Abel Smith and Mrs. John Dugdale.

The chief lady-in-waiting is the Mistress of the Robes, a much more formal position and one usually held by a duchess, now the Duchess of Grafton. She accompanies the Queen on very formal State occasions, such as the opening

of Parliament. The Duchess is usually visible in the background of photographs of the Queen at these events. One of
her tasks is to dress in a way distinctly less noticeable than
the Queen—it doesn't do to upstage the chief attraction. The
Duchess is the wife of the 11th Duke, and was born in 1920
as Anne Fortune-Smith, daughter of Captain Eric Smith.
She married the then Earl of Euston in 1946; he succeeded
to the dukedom in 1970. The Duchess was one of the
Queen's Ladies of the Bedchamber from 1953 to 1956, and
has been Mistress of the Robes since 1967. The office she
holds was a political appointment until the early 20th century, and the incumbent had to resign with each change of
government. The badge of office was a golden key until
Sarah, Duchess of Marlborough, Queen Anne's Mistress of
the Robes, refused to give it back when she was sacked. Now
the badge is a miniature of the Queen set in an oval brooch
of pearls.

     One other person, technically Staff rather than House-
hold, and who is probably closer to the Queen than anybody
outside her family, is Margaret McKay "Bobo" Macdonald,
titled "Queen's Dresser." Born in 1904, she has worked at
the palace as a maid, nanny and dresser since Elizabeth was
four years old, and has her own apartment on the top floor
of the north wing, directly over the Queen's Sitting Room.
Aside from members of her own family, the Queen regards
Miss Macdonald as her closest confidante, a trust "Bobo" has
never betrayed. The rest of the palace employees, from
Household to Staff, are in considerable awe of her, fully
aware of the relationship she enjoys with the Queen. She
refers to Elizabeth as "my little lady."

     Officials and Clerks are the middle-range employees;
Staff are the maids, footmen (sort of male maids) and other
generally blue-collar employees. All of these people, as well
as Household, must sign pledges of secrecy at the outset of
their employment in the palace. The Queen doesn't want

former employees writing books about what they "saw in the palace," which she feels not only invades her family's privacy, but usually distorts and trivializes the workings of the monarchy.

The Queen also has a full-fledged Household in Scotland, headed by the Hereditary Lord High Constable, the Earl of Erroll, and the Hereditary Master of the Household, the Duke of Argyll. The Scottish nobility is well represented in this establishment, which has many of the same departments as its English counterpart. Another distinctive Scottish Household organization is the Queen's Bodyguard for Scotland, known as the Royal Company of Archers and headed by the Captain General and Gold Stick for Scotland, the Earl of Stair. The former Prime Minister, Sir Alec Douglas-Home (now Lord Home of the Hirsel) is a member.

Besides the Queen's Household, other members of the royal family have their own separate establishments. The Household of the Duke of Edinburgh includes a Private Secretary, Lord Rupert Neville; an Assistant Private Secretary; an equerry, an extra equerry and two temporary equerries; and a chief clerk and accountant. Of course, in the larger sense, Prince Philip shares his wife's Household, and their combined organization is far larger than the next largest Household, that of the Queen Mother.

Prince Charles's Household is headed by his Private Secretary, Edward Adeane. Princess Anne's Private Secretary, Major N. S. Lawson, is in charge of her four ladies-in-waiting and a personal secretary. Princess Margaret has a Treasurer, Sir Francis Legh, and a Private Secretary, Lord Napier. She also has a lady-in-waiting and eight extra ladies-in-waiting, among whom is Mrs. Alastair Aird, wife of the Queen Mother's Comptroller.

Other royal family members with official Households are the Duke and Duchess of Gloucester, Princess Alice of Gloucester, the Duke and Duchess of Kent, Princess Alexandra, and Prince and Princess Michael of Kent. The Michaels' establishment is the smallest—they get by with just a Private Secretary, Sir Peter Scott.

In addition to the royal employees are the military and semi-military bodies which "guard" the Queen while adding splendor and color to British life. (The actual personal security of the Queen and her family is a function of the Metropolitan police which assigns detective-bodyguards to protect them.)

The oldest royal bodyguard is the Honorable Corps of Gentlemen-at-Arms, and is called the Queen's "nearest guard" as it is the closest in attendance on the monarch, and has been since it was founded by Henry VIII in 1509 as the "Gentlemen Pensioners." The present title was granted by William IV. Its 28 members serve the Queen on all State occasions and are usually seen at large palace functions. A number of peers are counted among the Corps. Its Captain is the Lord Denman, who recently replaced the Baroness Llewelyn-Davies in the position.

Another group is the Queen's Bodyguard of the Yeomen of the Guard, who today perform ceremonial duties—attending receptions of State visitors, accompanying the Royal Coach to and from Parliament at the annual openings, distributing the Maundy money, and so on. Their uniform, the most picturesque of any military body in the world (perhaps excepting the Vatican's Swiss Guard), includes scarlet doublets embroidered with royal emblems, black velvet Tudor hats and white ruffs. The Captain is the Lord Sandys, a former lieutenant in the Royal Scots Greys. The Yeomen are often confused with the Warders of the Tower (the famous "Beefeaters"), a separate body which participates in no State ceremonial, but serves as keepers of England's oldest royal palace, the Tower of London.

Closely associated with the palace are the Regular Army regiments which have direct responsibility for militarily guarding the Queen and the metropolis of London: the

Household Cavalry and the Foot Guards, together known as the Household Division. It is in these regiments that service has been for decades practically de rigueur for the titled and aristocratic young bloods of Britain's great families. The Household Cavalry, officially the senior units of the British Army, consists of the Life Guards and the Blues and Royals, the latter a 1969 merging of the Royal Horse Guards and the Royal Dragoons. The Queen is Colonel-in-Chief of the Household Division. The daily guard changing ceremony at the Horse Guards in Whitehall is a major London tourist attraction. Their splendid uniforms with plumed steel helmets, scarlet or blue tunics, tight white trousers and glistening black knee-high boots with flaring flanges have been a familiar London sight for decades.

A curiously unasked question is why a guard should be mounted at Horse Guards in the first place—it's nowhere near the Queen. In days past, when the Court resided in Whitehall Palace, the Horse Guards (which is a building) served as its ceremonial entrance, so the guard was theoretically protecting the sovereign. In Britain, nothing is so sacrosanct as royal ceremonial, so 300 years after the court moved from Whitehall, Whitehall is still being "guarded."

The five regiments of the Foot Guards, termed the Brigade of Guards, consist of the Grenadier, Coldstream, Scots, Irish and Welsh Guards, the first two being senior. Their formal dress uniforms are, at first glance, identical, with scarlet tunics, blue trousers, and the brigade's trademark, tall bearskin ("buskin") hats. (The hats of the officers are made out of the finer skins of female bears; the enlisted men get by with the coarser and less elegant male skins.) The small differences in the expensive uniforms are in the badges, the grouping of the tunic buttons and the color of the hat plumes: the Grenadiers' badge is a flaming grenade, the buttons are evenly spaced, and the hat has a white plume; the Coldstream have a Garter star, buttons in pairs, and a red plume; the Scots a thistle, buttons in threes, and no plume; the Irish a shamrock, buttons in fours, and blue cut feathers; and the Welsh a leek, buttons in two groups of five, and a longer plume of white cut feathers. The Brigade of Guards is world famous for its guard duties at the royal residences in London. Formerly they stood outside the railings at Buckingham Palace, a tempting target for tourists who tried to get them to break their rigid stance, but they are now less picturesquely albeit more safely stationed inside the railings.

The most splendid ceremony involving the Household Division is the annual Queen's Birthday Parade in June, known as the Trooping the Colour (often incorrectly referred to by Americans as the "Trooping *of* the Colour"), a custom dating to 1805 and continuing almost without interruption ever since. The Birthday Parade is as stunningly costumed, choreographed and sound-tracked as an MGM musical. It takes place in Horse Guards Parade (the large open space behind the Horse Guards), and is the major annual Court ceremonial. All seven regiments pass by the Queen, who is sitting atop her horse sidesaddle (never astride, considered vulgar for a woman, much less the Queen—as a young girl, the Queen was taught to ride sidesaddle since her grandfather the King didn't like women to even learn to ride astride), and wearing a special feminine version of one of the five Foot Guards' uniforms, rotating the uniforms each year to be fair to all.

The Queen is a stickler for absolute perfection in the ceremony which she has performed so many times, beginning after the War when she was deputized for her ailing father. Especially punctilious about spacing, she once chastised an officer whose horse was encroaching on her: "Actually, Captain, I *think* they've come to see *me*."

Another classification of court personages are the Great Officers of State. The royal Household was originally the center of Britain's government, and the ranking members of the Court were the sovereign's closest advisers. By virtue of their status they were, in effect, the principal executives and administrators of the country. When ministerial responsibility for executive acts slowly came into effect, some of the leading Household officers became members of the political administration, completely divorced from Household duties. These officers are the Lord Chancellor (who is Britain's highest judicial officer, as well as President of the House of Lords, and who vacates his office with a change in government), Lord President of the Council, the Lord Privy Seal, the Secretary of State (now divided among several ministers), the Lord Great Chamberlain, and the Earl Marshal. (Two others, the Lord High Steward and the Lord High Constable, are created only for the single day of a coronation.) While none any longer has duties connected with the royal Household, the last two still function in connection with royal ceremonial.

The office of the Lord Great Chamberlain goes back to Henry I in the 12th century. It had been vested in the family of the earls of Oxford, but when the line died out in the 17th century, utter confusion reigned as to which collateral branch of the family should hold the office. Finally, in 1902, the Court of Claims settled it in a truly Solomonaic manner—it would be held by differing claiming families in alternate reigns: first, the marquesses of Cholmondeley, and then the marquesses of Lincolnshire sharing it with the earls of Ancaster. So, a Cholmondeley held it under Edward VII, then a Lincolnshire under George V, a Cholmondeley again under Edward VIII, two Ancasters—the 5th and 6th earls— under George VI, and a Cholmondeley—the 6th marquess— under the present Queen. When Charles III comes to the throne, the holder will be Lord Carrington, descendant of the younger brother of the Marquess of Lincolnshire, whose only son died in World War I. (The present Lord Carrington is Mrs. Thatcher's Foreign Secretary.) What with all this wrangling to get the job, you'd think it were a really important one. Actually, the duties of the Lord Great Chamberlain are practically nonexistent, but for the record, he does stand just to the sovereign's immediate left at a coronation and gets to fasten the clasp on the sovereign's robe.

The Earl Marshaldom of England is held by the family of the Duke of Norfolk, England's "premier" peer (meaning the oldest peerage in the highest rank—a dukedom). The duke, as Earl Marshal, is head of the College of Arms (the court of last resort for questions armorial), and is responsible for the arrangements at coronations and State funerals. The duke is a Roman Catholic, but still stage-manages these High Church of England ceremonies. During the last two coronations, the office was held by the 16th duke, famous for his cherry-cheeked visage and the no-nonsense seriousness with which he carried out his duties. He died in January 1975, and was succeeded by his distant cousin, Lord Beaumont, also a Roman Catholic, who is in line to take on the direction of King Charles III's coronation.

This great panoply of characters not only makes the monarchy run as if it were on greased skids, but it also provides the pageantry which marks the special flair of Britain's Crown. The public sees only the incredibly smoothly functioning ceremonial side of royalty; hidden from view is the mundane bureaucracy and plain hard work that makes the whole thing come off.

In all likelihood, England's Queen is the world's busiest monarch. Overwork was in large part responsible for her father's early death, and today the Queen's many chores are far greater than those her father had to face. She is, in fact, busier than any of her civil servants, constantly presented with endless piles of paperwork and endless rounds of public duties and engagements.

Queen Elizabeth II is awakened at 8:00 every morning by the sound of Bobo Macdonald knocking on her door. Miss Macdonald takes a tray of tea in to her, and together they decide on the one or many costumes the Queen will wear during the day. If any kind of formal ceremonies or gala evening engagements are on the schedule, the task becomes a fairly complicated one. The Queen knows that people are disappointed if she wears something that has been seen too often or too recently, this being the main reason her wardrobe is so vast.

Often Philip comes from his bedroom to join his wife for breakfast, during which (like the Queen Mother) they'll be serenaded by the shrill honking of bagpipes being played by a British Army pipe major. Queen Victoria started this tradition, and it is now firmly embedded in the rubric of royal usage.

Much of the Queen's work is done at her desk in her sitting room–study in Buckingham Palace. The study itself was her mother's during the last reign, Philip being given George VI's study, but the Queen has continued to use the desk her father worked on. Each weekday at 10:00, the Queen's Private Secretary, Sir Philip Moore, brings stacks of correspondence and State papers to her, entering with a slight bow of the head, his one formal obeisance of the day. She sees other Household department heads on an as-needed basis—the head chef, for instance, to check the menu before a State banquet.

Sir Philip, together with his staff, actually manages the Queen and the British monarchy, and works out a schedule with her from thousands of invitations received each year to attend every imaginable kind of event, only a relatively small number of which she can possibly accept. Personal letters to the Queen, specially coded by the sender on the envelope with a cipher made known to them by the palace, are opened personally by Elizabeth, and often answered by her in her own hand. Other mail has been summarized for her, and is then sent to appropriate persons to be answered—many to the government departments concerned, the bulk to ladies-in-waiting for a courtly reply ("I am afraid that there is no question of your having an audience . . ."). Everything is answered except obvious crank mail, which is sent along to Scotland Yard.

If the Queen has no outside appointments, her staff schedules three audiences with her each morning. There's never a shortage of persons requesting or expecting audiences with their monarch. She sees retiring civil servants, distinguished foreign visitors to Britain, or perhaps one of her subjects who has been responsible for some worthy deed. The Queen has been known to ask some of these people to stay on to lunch with her if they have had the last audience in the morning.

Every Tuesday evening when she is in London, the Queen receives her Prime Minister. These were fairly starchy affairs in Queen Victoria's day, when it came as something of a revelation that she allowed Disraeli to *sit* during the meetings. There was certainly no similar dispensation for her bête noire, Gladstone. Now the meetings are simpler but still confidential tête-à-têtes, with the PM bringing the sovereign up to date on all national and international matters of importance. The Queen's relationship with Harold Wilson was known to be particularly warm. He once described her as "the one working colleague to whom I could take my problems without fear that I might later be stabbed in the back."

One task the Queen will never be talked into is holding a press conference, or, for that matter, even giving an interview, knowing full well that if she does the requests will become a deluge. She has absolutely never done such a thing, and, according to the palace, absolutely never will. Others of her family—except the Queen Mother—have done so, but *never* the Queen.

The most important and time-consuming part of her daily desk work, taking anywhere up to three hours every day, is "doing the boxes," those famous red metal containers whose contents include diplomatic communiqués, minutes of cabinet meetings, official government secrets, bills passed by both houses which will become law only after she signs them—at the top, by the way, rather than at the bottom in the manner of American presidents. Although this reading of State papers is symbolic rather than functional in the sense that the Queen has no responsibility for her government's decisions, her conscientious daily attention to the "boxes" for 28 years, a task she has undertaken with the utmost serious-ness, has probably made her the best-informed person in her kingdom. For the last several years, the Queen has shared seeing the boxes and discussing their contents with her eldest son, a privilege she has never extended to anyone else—not even her husband.

Nearly everything in official British life is carried out in the Queen's name—the government is "Her Majesty's Gov-ernment," not "the British Government." This same princi-ple holds true for nearly all facets of the nation—justice, armed forces, civil service, diplomacy, police, postal ser-vices—all functions exercised in the name of Queen Eliza-beth II. Like so many activities and functions in which her name is invoked, these are also representative of the supreme authority of the State, but there are also many major acts of government which require the actual participation of the Queen.

In one of her most symbolically important duties, the Queen summons, prorogues (ends sessions), and dissolves Parliament at the request of the Prime Minister. Normally, she opens each new session in November with a speech from the throne which outlines the government's program for the next year. (There used to be only one throne on the dais, and Prince Philip sat on a smaller seat below; now there is a matching throne for him on the Queen's left, but just to keep things in proper perspective, Elizabeth's gilded chair is raised two inches on small blocks—barely noticeable, but evidently considered necessary.) Although the speech is drafted in personal terms, it is composed entirely by the Prime Minister's office, and the Queen must read it exactly as written. A few years ago she complained to her ministers, "Why can't you give me something more readable?" The speech has since been freer of ministerial babble. If the sovereign is unable to be present for the ceremony, a rare circumstance, the Lord Chancellor reads the speech. The State opening of the British legislature is accompanied by the ritual pageantry of the Queen's drive to Westminster in the Irish State Coach and the preliminary search of the Houses of Parliament to make sure nobody has hidden any explosives in an attempt to blow it up, this last bit in symbolic memory of Guy Fawkes but becoming a more realistic possibility every year. The entire ceremony of the State opening is in the charge of the Earl Marshal.

By far the most *potentially* important power of the British monarch lies in the right of the throne to appoint the Prime Minister. In nearly all cases, the appointment is merely a pro forma confirmation of the leader of the party commanding the most votes or a working majority of the House of Commons. Only once so far in Queen Elizabeth II's reign has there been some likelihood of her own personal choice coming into the matter. When Sir Anthony Eden (later Lord Avon) resigned as Prime Minister in 1957 because of illness and loss of personal prestige over the Anglo-French debacle in Egypt the year before, there were two leading personalities in the Conservative Party. The man the country expected would be named Prime Minister was R. A. "Rab"

Butler; the man the Queen actually named was Harold Macmillan, the Cabinet's favorite. There is little question that the Queen's mind was decided by the advice of Tory leaders Lord Salisbury and Sir Winston Churchill, but to the British public it looked as though she had exceeded the bounds of constitutional monarchy by going against the wishes of the majority. Time proved the probable wisdom of the selection, as Macmillan was able to almost miraculously regroup the Suez-damaged Conservative Party to bring about a great electoral victory in 1959. But the lesson has been learned—the Queen reached the nadir of her popularity by becoming enmeshed in party politics. Since then, the appointment of each Prime Minister has been routine and preordained, but it is extremely unlikely that the Queen would ever again allow herself to be used in any remotely similar political situation.

In 1974, she headed off Edward Heath's attempt to form a precarious Conservative/Liberal coalition government after his party had been defeated in the General Election. Going strictly by the book—the British Constitution—she was required to name as Prime Minister the leader of the Commons' only working majority, Harold Wilson of the Labour Party, which is exactly what she did.

A provision of the British constitutional system is that new Parliamentary elections must be called after a government has been in office for five years. This is the one piece of legislation over which the House of Lords has absolute veto power, as opposed to mere power to delay. Should a government attempt to circumvent this law, the Lords would undoubtedly veto the bill. In an attempt to get around the Lords' veto, the Prime Minister could either create enough new peers to carry the matter, or else intimidate or otherwise force the peers to vote in favor. Here the sovereign could legitimately use the royal veto, her legal right, but not actually invoked since the time of Queen Anne. If circumstances came to this, Britain's democracy would probably be on the verge of collapse, but the Queen's veto could at least serve to deny *legitimacy* to a potential dictator—something dictators have historically sought. If the sovereign were ignored, it would certainly serve to reveal the true proportions of the government's illegal intent. Admittedly, this scenario is remote, but if it were ever to occur, it is only the monarch who would be in a legal position to save Britain from totalitarianism.

Another of the Queen's myriad duties is to preside over meetings of her Privy Council. This group of high-ranking Britons is a feeble remnant of the powerful Tudor body which carried out the bidding of the first Elizabeth. Today, the almost entirely ceremonial council is made up of 300 members (although three make a working quorum), all with the title "Right Honorable." The roster, which includes the top-ranking members of the government of the day, reads like a *Who's Who* of the British establishment; the initials "P.C." after a councilor's name indicate infinite status in Britain. The Council formally declares wars and affirms treaties by the formula of "Queen in Council." It grants royal charters after approval by Parliament and gives formal assent to many other legislative actions. At meetings, everyone stands, including the Queen; this was thought by an early king to ensure the quick conclusion of business. Britain's addiction to historical precedents knows few bounds.

This kind of royal ceremonial has always aroused widespread popular interest, and is an extremely important factor in the relationship between the Queen and the public, a relationship that is fostered by many means, including modern mass communications media. The "Royal Family" film, for instance, first shown on British television in June 1969, and aired in the United Kingdom four times subsequently, as well as in the United States and most of Europe, did much to demystify the Queen and her family. There is a constant stream of royal film, variety shows, and appearances at benefits for charity as well as visits to schools, universities, hospitals and factories.

The Queen is well known for her attendance at many important sporting events, and as an owner and breeder of thoroughbred racehorses she often watches her horses race. Besides the Derby at Epsom, she annually attends the Royal Ascot meeting. Here the royal family has since 1711 secluded themselves in the Royal Enclosure, admission to which has become one of the most sought-after prizes in what is left of Britain's high society. The relative democratization of the Enclosure has in recent years prompted the royal family's further entrenchment into what is called the Queen's Lawn, a small section within the Enclosure into which the crème de la crème can still maintain an appropriate distance from the merely rich.

In addition to the fact that she is head of all three armed services, the Queen is Colonel-in-Chief of several regiments and corps in the United Kingdom and other Commonwealth countries. Apart from regular visits to units of the services, her military duties include the performance of the annual Trooping the Colour. By the way, she salutes superbly, the only woman to do so, according to one retired Field Marshal.

One form of ritual the Queen no longer has to put up with is the Presentation Party. These parties, which Elizabeth dispensed with in 1958, were the successors to the Courts and Levees which were last held in 1939. "Courts" were the grand and colorful evening balls in which young women, usually rich and always well-connected, made their debut at Court; "Levees" were sort of a masculine equivalent. After the War, new economic realities brought about the much smaller Presentation Parties, which were in turn finally chucked after becoming little more than a racket. The idea that a privileged class of young women could be made acceptable at Court (that is to say, eligible to be allowed to be in the "official" presence of the King or Queen) by the formula of these "presentations" became increasingly distasteful to a country in which such highly visible class barriers were being broken down. Since 1958, an invitation to one of the Queen's huge Royal Garden Parties is considered the same as a court debut for those who still attach much importance to the age-old custom.

About 8,000 guests are invited to each of the Garden Parties, which are held three times every summer in the Buckingham Palace gardens. Technically, the invitations are "commands," and are issued by the Lord Chamberlain in the Queen's name. (Only the Queen's and the Queen Mother's social invitations carry the heady cachet of "command" status; all others of the royal family are merely "invitations.") Each is sent out accompanied by an admission card which states that acknowledgment isn't necessary unless the invitee can't attend, in which case the admission card must be returned to the Lord Chamberlain.

The parties are now almost democratic compared to the society "garden breakfasts" initiated by Queen Victoria in 1868. Starting at 3:15, and ending a bit less than three hours later, the guests take tea (a modest Indian leaf) and buttered bread and chocolate cupcakes (supplied by Lyons, a rather down-market catering firm). A band is playing, mostly glutinous Broadway show melodies. The Queen doesn't actually mingle with the throng, but moves along a carefully cleared and defined route, with courtiers acting as accompanying linebackers to keep her from getting mobbed. Most of her family, including the cousins, are doing the same thing along their carefully defined routes. There's never a shortage of party-goers who want to be presented to the Queen, and who get to exchange a few words with her after a bow or curtsy and handshake (the Queen uses only her gloved fingertips; otherwise, with her yearly volume of handshakes, she'd have a crippled hand). For the person presented the short exchange will most likely be a memory lasting a life-time.

Another of the Queen's continuing duties is travel, both at home and overseas. Hundreds of royal visits to every part of the United Kingdom keep the Queen in remarkably close touch with the mood of her country while serving to person-alize and popularize the monarchy, largely through the as-tonishing personal charisma of the sovereign. In most cases these visits center around a local event of great significance, at least to those involved—the opening of a new hospital or perhaps an agricultural show. If the Queen can't conve-niently be driven in one of the royal Rolls's, she travels either on the royal train, with her own RAF detachment, or on the HMY *Britannia*.

Although British Rail provides the royal cars, which cost several thousand pounds each year to maintain, they are attached to regular trains, and the Queen and her family pay the normal mileage charges for their personal travel. Two new "day saloons" for the Queen and Prince Philip have re-cently been built at a cost of £500,000. The cars have a kitchen, dining room, bedrooms, and a sophisticated com-munications system. The decor is quietly luxurious.

The Queen's Flight was created in 1936 by King Ed-ward VIII (as the King's Flight, of course) to provide for the royal family's official duties and visits by air. (It turned out to be his one innovation to survive his reign.) The RAF maintains what is called the "Purple Airway" for the Flight, a safety space 10 miles wide, 4,000 feet deep, and from which all other planes are banned for one half hour on either side of the royal plane's passing. Based at Benson, in Oxfordshire, the Flight is equipped with a VC-10, three Hawker Siddeley "Andover" jet airliners and two Westland "Wessex" helicop-ters. It requires about 140 people—RAF officers and enlisted personnel and civilians, and now costs about £1,800,000 per year to operate. It is provided without charge to the royal family. The Queen, Queen Mother and Duke of Edinburgh are entitled to use it whenever they wish; at the Queen's discretion, it is also made available to other members of the royal family, but only for official duties. The Flight is also used by the Prime Minister and certain other high-ranking ministers, the service chiefs and visiting heads of state. Incidentally, the Queen and Prince Charles, as monarch and heir apparent, never fly on the same aircraft together.

One of the most glamorous duties of the sovereign is to act as host to the heads of state of Commonwealth and other countries when they visit the United Kingdom. When a State visit (only one of which is usually accorded to any one head of state during his term in office) is involved, guests stay at Buckingham Palace, Windsor Castle or the Palace of Holyroodhouse. Their entertainment includes magnificent banquets, receptions, often a special ballet or opera performance, and visits to places of significance to the visitor. On other non-State occasions when these visitors come to Britain on private trips, they are nearly always received by the Queen and often by other members of the royal family as well. Receptions and luncheons are frequently held for other distinguished foreign visitors.

The overseas tours which the Queen and Duke of Edinburgh make together, today one of their most important functions, fall into two categories. There are visits to other Commonwealth countries, made at the invitation of the host government; and there are State visits to countries outside the Commonwealth made at the invitation of a foreign leader and accepted on the advice of the British government. (The Queen never makes private visits to any country until after she has made a State visit.) Most members of the royal family have visited foreign countries as the Queen's representative. Princess Alexandra's 1974 visit to Poland was the first by a member of the royal family to a Warsaw Pact country.

The family has been given thousands of presents, many extremely lavish, on these trips, and in contrast to American attitudes toward gifts to the President, British royals keep them. On her 1979 Middle East tour, the oil sheiks presented the Queen with $2,000,000 worth of jewelry.

Parenthetically, since passports are issued in her name, the Queen doesn't need one. All the rest of her family, including her husband, carry them.

On a purely private basis, the Queen spends several weekends each year with close friends, creating an odd social situation which today must be unique to British royalty. The host must always surrender his place to the Queen, he himself being seated on her right at dinner. Among the private homes the Queen and Duke of Edinburgh visit is that of their closest friends, 57-year-old Lord Rupert Neville and his wife, Anne. Lord Rupert is the younger brother and heir to the fifth Marquess of Abergavenny; Lady Anne is the daughter of the ninth Earl of Portsmouth.

In the summer of 1976, the Queen and her husband visited the United States in honor of the American bicentennial celebration. After touring Philadelphia, the couple were guests of President and Mrs. Ford at a State dinner in an air-conditioned tent erected over the White House rose garden. During the dancing afterward, Vice-President Rockefeller committed an act of lèse majesté by draping his arm around the Queen while chatting with her. She didn't take any obvious notice of it. As Princess Margaret puts it in her tone of acid hauteur, "My sister copes very well with presidents." Presumably, she copes equally well with vice-presidents.

Until recent years, the monarch was always officially entertained after a foreign tour at a formal dinner given by the Lord Mayor of the City of London. The idea was to celebrate a "safe homecoming." The present Queen has done away with this near insult to foreign hosts. It probably made some sense when Henry V was so entertained after his journey to Agincourt, but it certainly doesn't now.

On many of her stately foreign progresses, the Queen uses her yacht, HMY *Britannia*. The yacht, which is really a small ocean liner, was launched at Clydebank in 1953, and serves as an official and private residence for the sovereign and other members of the royal family when they make official visits overseas or are voyaging in home waters. It has been used as a floating honeymoon hotel twice—for Princess Margaret in 1960 and for Princess Anne in 1973. This sort of thing creates an instant furor in the British press, understandably, considering the ship costs well over £3,000,000 a year to operate. The sleek, 412-foot ship has a crew of 21 officers and 256 men (known as "Snotty Yachties" by the rest of the Royal Navy) in addition to the party of 30 or so of the Queen's staff who accompany her on voyages. Its permanent mooring is at Portsmouth on the Channel coast. The hull of *Britannia* is royal blue above and red below, with a gold band below the upper deck. The upper works are white with buff-colored funnel and masts.

The ship is a floating palace where the Queen can entertain heads of state, and where she can rest between engagements on the gruelingly busy foreign tours. It contains an elegant drawing room which can accommodate 200 guests, a large dining room and a movie theater. The Queen and Prince Philip each have a private sitting room, the Queen's with white walls and a moss-green carpet, the Prince's with a gray carpet and teak paneling. An elevator connects these rooms with their bedrooms one deck up. Overlooking the stern is a sun lounge where the Queen likes to have breakfast.

The crew of the *Britannia* wear sneakers to muffle their steps, in the interests of royal peace and quiet. Orders on the upper deck are given, insofar as possible, with hand signals for the same reason. To stifle public indignation at the huge sums spent on upkeep of this most exotic of royal perks, the government stresses the fact that *Britannia* in wartime could be hastily converted into a 235-bed hospital ship.

4

Status
TITLES AND SUCCESSION

Titles are a matter of never-ending confusion even to invet-erate royalty-watchers. Not one writer in a dozen seems able to get his royal nomenclature correct, either confusing a Maj-esty with a Royal Highness, a royal duke with a nonroyal duke, a Queen Consort with a Queen Regnant. This chapter will attempt to put some order to the subject of royal titles (the nonroyal titles system will be explained in the following chapter on the nobility), as well as to define how the two major systems of royal succession work. Confusing as the whole structure may seem, one has only to keep certain prin-ciples and rules firmly in mind, and order emerges from chaos. Indeed, without the ironclad rules governing it, the system simply wouldn't work. The mechanism which has kept the gears from being stripped is rules; that which has brought about difficulties has been deviation from the rules. Follow closely, and it all comes clear.

A cardinal principle of kingship that is constant in all kingdoms is that the throne is never vacant—"The King is dead, long live the King." What this means is simply that a new sovereign succeeds to the throne at the instant his predecessor dies, or what is less likely, abdicates. What *is* different from country to country is the matter of eligibility to succeed to the throne. The primary distinction involves whether or not the kingdom follows the "Salic law," a legal provision which prohibits a woman from inheriting the throne. Of the seven European kingdoms, three of the four non-Salic thrones now happen to be occupied by women— Great Britain, Denmark and The Netherlands. Sweden has just joined them by removing its male-only proviso; Norway may not be far behind. Only Spain and Belgium, the two Roman Catholic kingdoms, show no sign of changing the royal inheritance laws.

There are factors other than sex which can affect the British succession laws—religion and morganatic marriage are two examples. But in the normal course of events, the line of inheritance to the Throne of Great Britain is led by the sovereign's sons in descending order of age, followed by his or her daughters in order of age. In the absence of children (or "issue," as historians and genealogists call royal offspring), the sovereign's brothers in order of age are next in line, followed by sisters in order of age. In the absence of brothers or sisters, the succession would go in the same order of sex and age to the siblings of the sovereign's father (assuming that it was the father of the sovereign who preceded him to the throne; if the sovereign's mother had been monarch, then the succession would of course go to the maternal uncles and aunts).

This line can be extended to great-uncles and great-aunts, and so on. But it is relatively rare for anyone beyond the sovereign's child or grandchild to inherit a throne. The reason is that as soon as a person in the line of succession has a child, that child precedes whoever was next in line. This means that if the king's heir predeceases him, he (the king) would be succeeded by that heir's child before he would by his own next child or other heir. This has happened comparatively often—both Queen Victoria and Sweden's present king were the grandchildren, not children, of monarchs; their own fathers died before their grandfathers.

As can be seen, the major factor affecting this direct order of succession is sex. All sons, regardless of whether their sisters are older, precede those sisters in succession. A new Swedish constitutional provision in which the monarch's children will inherit the throne *solely* in order of age and without regard to sex is the first time in European history a sister will be able to be legally ahead of her legitimate brother in the line of succession. (This will occur with Sweden's next monarch: of the present king's two children, the sister is older than her brother.)

Now we'll see how these laws of succession have actually affected the inheritance of England's Crown, starting with King George I, who came to the throne through the most circuitous set of circumstances in the country's history since Henry VII. George's immediate predecessor, Queen Anne, was childless and the last acceptable Protestant of her House. Under the provisions of the Act of Settlement of 1701, which was designed to ensure Protestant succession, Queen Anne's successors were to be the Electress Sophia of Hanover (being the eldest branch of the Protestant line), a niece of Charles I, and her Protestant descendants. Since Sophia died shortly before Queen Anne's death, it was her eldest son who inherited the English Crown as King George I.

George was in turn succeeded by his eldest son, George II. George II's eldest son, Frederick, Prince of Wales, died nine years before he did, so Frederick's eldest son succeeded as George III. (Note here that George III preceded any of his father's brothers.) George III was followed by his eldest son, George IV. George IV had only one legitimate child (naturally, any illegitimate children don't count), Princess Charlotte, who would have succeeded him as Queen, but she died in childbirth 13 years before her father's death. If her child had lived, he would have succeeded to the throne on his grandfather's death.

Since George IV had no living descendants, children or grandchildren, he was followed by his next younger brother, the Duke of Clarence, as King William IV. William's heir, since he had no legitimate children, was his next younger brother, the Duke of Kent. The Duke had only one child, Princess Victoria. Because the Duke of Kent died before King William, it was Victoria who became the new sovereign on her uncle's death.

Had there been a Salic law in effect in England, it is at this point where history would have made a considerable change. Victoria would not have been eligible to succeed; rather her uncle, the wicked Duke of Cumberland, as the Duke of Kent's next younger brother, would have become king. Instead, the Duke of Cumberland inherited the Kingdom of Hanover (upgraded in the meantime from an electorate), since the time of George I merged with the British Crown but which still adhered to the Salic law, thus making Victoria ineligible for its throne.

Queen Victoria's succession went in the perfectly ordinary way to her eldest son, Edward VII. His eldest son, the unmarried Duke of Clarence and Avondale, died before he did, so his second son succeeded as George V. George V's first son succeeded as Edward VIII. When this unmarried king abdicated, his next brother followed as George VI.

King George VI had two daughters, Elizabeth and Margaret, and no sons. There was a bit of ticklish business which flared up briefly at the time regarding the succession laws. In the British nobility system, age has no affect on inheritance rights of sisters; in the absence of brothers, they are considered co-heiresses, equal in law. Some legalists felt the principle applied to the Crown, as well. Parliament wisely decided this was nonsense, confirming the order of succession with elder sister followed by the younger. Consequently, Queen Elizabeth II followed her father to the Throne of England on his death in 1952.

All this leaves us with the succession to the British Throne today. Prince Charles, the Prince of Wales, is the Heir Apparent to the throne, "Crown Prince" if you will, although Britain has never used the terms "Crown Prince" or "Crown Princess," the titles used by some of the Continental monarchies. He is followed by his brothers, Andrew first, and then Edward. Princess Anne comes next, followed by her son, Peter Phillips (who is not a prince, the reason for which will be explained shortly). Since this exhausts the Queen's children and grandchildren, her next successor would be her sister, Princess Margaret, followed by her two children, David, Viscount Linley, and Lady Sarah Armstrong-Jones. As the Queen has no more sisters, we have to go back to the line of her father's next younger brother, the late Duke of Gloucester. His unmarried eldest son, Prince William, was killed in an air accident, so his second son, the present Duke of Gloucester, is next in line, followed in turn by his son, Alexander, the Earl of Ulster, and daughters, Lady Davina and Lady Rose Windsor. Next is the Kent family, the youngest brother of King George VI. The present Duke of Kent, who succeeded his father the first Duke of Kent in 1942, is followed by his two sons, George, the Earl of St. Andrews, and Lord Nicholas Windsor, and his daughter, Lady Helen Windsor. Prince Michael of Kent formerly stood next in line, but since his marriage to a Roman Catholic, he has had to renounce his succession rights. However, his son, Lord Frederick, is still eligible to succeed, and thus follows Lady Helen. Next is the Duke of Kent's only sister, Princess Alexandra, and her children in order, Mr. James Ogilvy and Miss Marina Ogilvy. Exhausting the Kent line, we go to the late King's only sister, the late Princess Mary, Princess Royal. Her son, the Earl of Harewood, is followed by his sons, David, Viscount Lascelles, and the Honorable James, Jeremy and Mark Lascelles (the latter son is by the earl's second marriage). Then comes the earl's younger brother, the Honorable Gerald Lascelles, and his son, Mr. Henry Lascelles.

This completes the descendants of King George V, and of course has long since exhausted any realistic possibility of successors to the throne. But for the sake of further demonstrating the principle of succession, the list can quite easily be continued almost endlessly. The family of King George V's oldest sister, the Duchess of Fife, would be next in order. The present Duke of Fife heads that line. Next after the Fife family would be that of George V's youngest sister (the middle sister never married), Queen Maud of Norway, thus making Norway's present King Olav (that Queen's only child) next in succession. Having completed King Edward VII's descendants, we go back to the second son of Queen Victoria, and run through his descendants, then those of her third son and then fourth son. Next would be the descendants of her eldest daughter, the Empress Frederick of Germany, followed by the four families of the younger daughters. By this time, we have over 200 people living today. The order has long since become purely academic, but it does serve to illuminate the rigid order of succession to the British Throne.

To this point in the book, a good many different royal titles have been used. Let us now turn to sorting out these sometimes confusing terms and some of the fine points of status connected with them.

The terms "the sovereign" or "monarch" and "the Crown," although related, are quite distinct. The sovereign or monarch is the person on whom the Crown is constitutionally conferred, whereas the Crown, which represents not only the sovereign but his or her government as well, is the symbol of supreme executive power. The Crown "vests" in the king or queen (regnant), but in general its functions are exercised by ministers responsible to the kingdom's Parliament. In other words, European monarchies are ruled in the name of, not by, the sovereign.

Most European sovereigns have long strings of titles after their names, representing the accrued territories over which their ancestors have reigned or inherited through marriage. The rule seems to be that it's easier to gain titles than to give them up. Recent British monarchs have been quick to drop empty or lost titles, though; most lately, George VI gave up "Emperor of India" in 1947, reflecting his country's new relationship with its former "crown jewel."

A king, a queen regnant, and a queen consort are styled "Majesty," a form first used in Britain by Henry VIII. A queen consort retains the style after her husband's death. (Should a queen regnant abdicate, she would not retain it, but revert to "Royal Highness.") These are the only possible "majesties" in a kingdom. (The high point of the Buckingham Palace switchboard operator's day is when she puts the Queen through to the Queen Mother. "Your Majesty? Her Majesty, Your Majesty.")

A queen regnant's husband does not share his wife's style, but by royal decree rather than by right has the style of "Royal Highness." This follows the universal royal principle that a wife shares her husband's styles and title by right, but a husband does not share those of his wife.

In 1917, King George V decreed a new system of titles for the royal family, and it is followed to this day. Until 1917, a sovereign's sons, daughters and grandchildren by sons were styled "Royal Highness," while grandchildren by daughters were merely "Highnesses." He commanded that in future the style Royal Highness would go only to the sovereign's children and to the children of sons. The thinking was that Royal Highness should signify only those in the close line of succession. The style Highness (without the pre-

fix Royal) was allowed to lapse. (There is still one Highness
without the "Royal" in Britain, though. Queen Elizabeth II
conferred it on the Aga Khan in 1957.) The title Prince or
Princess (Majesty, Royal Highness, Honorable, and so forth,
are "styles"; King, Queen, Prince, Princess, and so forth, are
"titles") would apply in the same way to the sovereign's children and to grandchildren through sons.

This rule caused an obvious problem when Princess
Elizabeth was expecting her first child. According to the formula, the baby would be born without a royal style or title.
Since that was patently unthinkable, King George VI made
an exception to the rule in the case of his eldest daughter,
thus saving Prince Charles the ignominy of having been born
merely "the Earl of Merioneth," his father's secondary title.

In England today, Royal Highnesses in their own right
include the Queen's children, her sister, her cousins the
Dukes of Gloucester and Kent, Princess Alexandra of Kent
and Prince Michael of Kent. Until her recent death, the list
included the Queen's great-aunt, Princess Alice, Countess of Athlone (through her father, the youngest son of
Queen Victoria, and who was that monarch's last living
grandchild; Princess Alice was also the Queen's great-aunt by
marriage, being the widow of Queen Mary's brother). Princess Alice of Gloucester has the style and title through marriage, as do the wives of the present Dukes of Gloucester and
Kent and Prince Michael of Kent. The children of the Queen's
cousins have inherited neither the style of Royal Highness nor
the titles of Prince or Princess since they are only the great-
grandchildren of a king. The heirs to both the Duke of
Gloucester and the Duke of Kent use the secondary titles of
their fathers as courtesy titles, and will someday inherit their
fathers dukedoms, but as "ordinary" dukes rather than as
royal dukes.

Following the rule, Princess Margaret's children, as
grandchildren of a king through a daughter, are non-Royal
Highnesses, and thus have the styles and titles related to

their noble father, not their royal mother. If their father *weren't* a peer, the children would be simply Mr. and Miss Armstrong-Jones.

Recent history's most famous feud involving the granting (actually nongranting) of the style of Royal Highness is George VI's refusal to permit the newly created Duke of Windsor to share the royal style with his wife—*any* wife. The refusal was carefully and tactfully worded so as not to specifically exclude Mrs. Simpson by name, but rather *any* woman the ex-King might marry. But, of course, it was Mrs. Simpson that King George had in mind. The King reasoned that it was by no means certain that the Duke and Duchess would stay married for any lengthy period (after all, Mrs. Simpson had already been divorced twice), and neither the King, his ministers, nor the Dominion leaders wanted a woman divorced from a royal duke continuing as a royal duchess. Besides, if Wallis were to become a Royal Highness, so would any children she might have with the Duke, thereby eventually inheriting the Duke's titles. It was felt that this could have a clouding effect on future succession to the throne, even though the wording of the instrument of abdication had Edward giving up the throne for "Myself and My descendants."

The Duchess of Windsor never forgave this slight, blaming (rightly, as it turned out) the Queen—now Queen Mother—for making sure that neither her husband, the King, nor her daughter, the future Queen, would ever give in and let the Duchess have the coveted style. Wallis would in future speak of Queen Elizabeth as the "dowdy duchess" (referring to her York title) or the "monster of Glamis." The Duke even got into the name-calling game, calling his sister-in-law "that fat Scotch cook." In fairness to the Queen Mother, it should be said that this was probably the only ungenerous thing she ever did in her life. But she probably correctly deduced the throne cost her husband many years

of his life. For her part, the Duchess of Windsor will undoubtedly go to her grave not as Her Royal Highness, but
merely as "Her Grace," the style of any ordinary duke's
wife.

Most rules have exceptions, and the rule that royal status is inheritable only as far as the sovereign's grandson has
its one qualification, too. The style and title of Royal Highness and Prince go as far as *great*-grandson through the sovereign's eldest son, the Prince of Wales. In practice, this
doesn't happen very often, since by the time the Prince of
Wales has a grandson, he will usually have already ascended
the throne and no longer be Prince of Wales. But it has happened: Queen Victoria had three direct generations of male
heirs in her lifetime, the Prince of Wales (Edward VII), the
Duke of York (George V), and Prince Edward (Edward
VIII).

Only the sovereign's first son, or eldest surviving son,
or eldest son of a deceased eldest son, is called Heir Apparent. The only situation in which a female can be called the
Heiress Apparent is if she is the only child or eldest daughter
(without brothers) of a deceased Heir Apparent. For example,
if Prince Charles had one child, a daughter, but he were to
predecease his mother, that daughter would be Heiress Apparent to Queen Elizabeth II. None of Britain's six sovereign
queens has come to the throne this way. Mary I could have
been displaced by the birth of a child to her brother, Edward
VI. Elizabeth I followed that sister to the throne, one who
presumably could have had male heirs to displace her younger
sister. Mary II's accession was essentially political and
artificial. Anne followed her brother-in-law, William III, who
survived his co-sovereign wife, Mary II, by eight years. Victoria could have been displaced anytime prior to her accession
by a child born to her uncle, William IV. Elizabeth II could
have been displaced by a son born to her parents. In contrast,
nobody can displace an Heir (or Heiress) Apparent—only

Prince Charles's death would remove him from eventually inheriting the throne.

Any other heir, including daughters of the sovereign, brothers or nephews, can only be Heirs or Heiresses Presumptive, indicating a "presumption" that the sovereign might still have a son (or a daughter even, in the case of a brother or nephew being the Heir Presumptive). To illustrate, Princess Elizabeth was always Heiress Presumptive, and bore only the customary title of a daughter of the king, that of princess. In some European monarchies, the Heir Apparent has a special title, such as Prince of the Asturias in Spain or Duke of Brabant in Belgium. Crown Prince or Crown Princess is the commonest title for the heir being used in the remaining monarchies.

In Britain, the monarch's first son is born with the title Duke of Cornwall in the peerage of England, and Duke of Rothesay, Earl of Carrick, and Baron Renfrew in the peerage of Scotland, as well as Lord of the Isles and Great Steward of Scotland. If still only the son of the heir, he comes into these titles when his parent succeeds to the throne. He is also granted the titles of Prince of Wales and Earl of Chester, but these are subject to the monarch's wish, rather than by virtue of his status as Heir Apparent. They were conferred on Prince Charles in 1958, although he wasn't "vested" with the principality of Wales until 1969.

The wife of the Prince of Wales is Princess of Wales. The latter title has never been granted in its own right, although there was some agitation after the War to confer it on Princess Elizabeth. King George sensibly turned down the idea, partly out of tradition and partly because of the anomalous position regarding a title in which it would place the Princess's future husband. The children of a Prince and Princess of Wales are called Prince or Princess *Whatever* of Wales. (One thus never refers to Prince Charles as "Prince Charles of Wales.")

The matter of titles for the husbands of queens has caused all sorts of problems. Queen Margrethe of Demark's husband is called Prince Henrik of Denmark and former Queen Juliana's husband is simply Prince of The Netherlands, a title he will presumably retain as husband of the now-Princess Juliana. The husband of the present Queen of England has no title indicating his position as husband of the Queen, but instead was given the dukedom of Edinburgh as well as the earldom of Merioneth and barony of Greenwich by King George VI the day before his marriage to Princess Elizabeth. Through what was possibly an oversight, he wasn't at that time made a Prince of the United Kingdom (a lapse corrected in 1957), although most people had referred to him as "Prince Philip" since his marriage. (Even though he was born a Prince of Greece, he gave up the title when he was naturalized at the time of his engagement). The title of Prince Consort has only once been conferred—on Queen Victoria's husband, Prince Albert. Perhaps it was compensation for the Queen's inability to get a British dukedom approved for Albert. There is no reason to believe that Prince Philip will ever be given the title of Prince Consort, as he seems quite content to be known as Duke of Edinburgh.

An unprecedented situation will be that of the Duke of Edinburgh's status if he outlives his wife. There is, of course, no male equivalent to Queen Mother—certainly not "King Father." Most likely, Philip would rank officially (have "precedence") immediately after his eldest son and daughter-in-law, and before any children they might have. (Precedence, which denotes one's official order of place or importance, a legal standing in Britain as it is in most countries, is discussed in Chapter 5.)

Younger sons of England's monarchs are given royal dukedoms (and the formal style of "Most High, Most Mighty and Illustrious Prince" that goes with this kind of dukedom) on attaining their majority. Until they become dukes, these princes are neither peers nor noblemen, which is a matter of having a seat in the House of Lords (except for some of the Irish peerages). Only the oldest son is automatically born with or inherits a peerage on his father or mother's accession, but even he is not eligible to take his seat in the House of Lords until he is 21. The second son has traditionally been made Duke of York, and Prince Andrew will probably be so dubbed in due course. Prince Edward's dukedom could be one of several available titles, such as Duke of Sussex.

The sovereign's daughters have no special title other than Princess (a monarch's daughter is never made a duchess in her own right), except that the oldest daughter can be named Princess Royal at the monarch's choosing and if it's available. The title is not "created," but is individually granted by royal declaration. In 1931, Princess Mary was declared to be Princess Royal. The title is an honorific, unique to Britain, and first used officially during the reign of George II (the title had been used once before—by Princess Mary, the daughter of Charles I—but only unofficially); it is granted to the sovereign's eldest daughter for her lifetime. The thinking behind the bestowal of the classier title at the time was that the eldest daughter is alone inheritable to the throne on the failure of the sovereign to produce a son, and should therefore be more "respected" than any of her younger sisters. (One can imagine King George II's oldest daughter burning a good deal of midnight oil to think *that* one up, but it worked since she talked her father into it, and naturally it has since become hallowed by time.) Princess Mary (the Countess of Harewood) has been the only daughter of a sovereign to be named Princess Royal who had no younger sisters, a seeming contradiction to the logic which first prompted this special honor. There can never be two Princesses Royal at the same time, so the holder must die before a new one is made. The position has been vacant since Princess Mary's death in 1965. Princess Anne is eligible to receive the title, but the Queen has not yet bestowed it on her daughter. Speculation as to the reasons are that the Queen may sense giving purely honorific titles to her family may not be in the spirit of the times and that, in any event, bestowing any additional titles on her testy daughter would be looked upon as excessive by the majority of her subjects.

The position of Queen Mother is interesting. To be Queen Mother, one can't merely have been the king or queen regnant's mother, but must have been the queen consort herself before her son or daughter came to be monarch. (It goes without saying that the queen regnant never becomes Queen Mother herself; in the case of a queen regnant abdicating, such as Holland's Juliana, she would revert to being a princess, as did Juliana.) Queen Victoria's mother was not Queen Mother, because her husband had never been king. The Queen Mother's precedence comes directly after that of the Queen and the Duke of Edinburgh, and ahead of Prince Charles. (Generally royal precedence follows the order of succession to the throne, but the cases of Prince Philip and the Queen Mother's relative precedence are obvious exceptions.)

Confusion often arises over the difference between the titles "Queen Mother" and "Queen Dowager." The difference can be subtle. An English queen is one of only three legal categories: Queen Regnant, Queen Consort or Queen Dowager. (The term "Queen Mother" is an informal title.) Elizabeth II is the first, the Queen Mother was the second while her husband was king, and is now the third. But while a Queen Mother is always a Queen Dowager, the reverse isn't necessarily so. If a Queen Consort were childless, and if, for example, her nephew or niece succeeded her late husband to the throne, she would still be Queen Dowager, but not Queen Mother. The most recent example was Queen Adelaide, King William IV's widow, who became Queen Dowager when her niece Victoria became Queen Regnant.

There was no Queen Mother since Victoria's mother, the Duchess of Kent, had never been a Queen Consort.

Of course, a Queen Dowager doesn't *have* to use any other title than "Queen" followed by her own name. Queen Alexandra chose to be known as just that after her husband's death. Queen Mary simply didn't like the titles Queen Mother or Queen Dowager, preferring to be called just "Queen Mary" during the reigns of her sons and granddaughter. Queen Elizabeth chose to be known as the Queen Mother because of her perfectly understandable wish to avoid confusion with her daughter, the new Queen Elizabeth II. However, on King George VI's death, Queen Elizabeth The Queen Mother ceased instantly to be known simply as "the Queen," a usage then reserved solely for her daughter.

Another fine point in dealing with royal titles concerns the use of the article "the." A prince or princess who is a child of the monarch ("Prince or Princess of the Blood Royal") rates its use in their formal title. Thus, "The Prince Andrew" or "The Princess Anne." Furthermore, it must be capitalized. Not so for a cousin—just "Prince Michael of Kent," not "The Prince Michael of Kent." The rule also applies to the Queen's mother—the correct formal title is "Queen Elizabeth The Queen Mother."

Members of the royal family have both family and house names, although they don't use "last names." Prince Albert's *family* name was Wettin, although he came from the *house* of Saxe-Coburg-Gotha. Following the normal course in which children take their father's name, the royal family therefore changed from being Hanovers to Saxe-Coburg-Gothas when Edward VII succeeded his mother. (Albert's family name was conveniently forgotten.) This was the state of the royal family's name when George V succeeded Edward VII. But by 1917, Britain was at war with Germany, so pressure was put on George to change the Germanic Saxe-Coburg-Gotha for something English. The reasons were similar to those that prompted Americans to call sauerkraut "liberty cabbage" during the same unfortunate period. After thinking about it for a while, he chose the name "Windsor," partly because it had been the home of English monarchs for centuries and partly because it sounded so well—and un-German. George's cousin, the Kaiser, was provoked by the change to make his witty remark about going to see a Berlin production of *The Merry Wives of Saxe-Coburg-Gotha.*

At the same time, the King asked his English relations with German names or titles to change theirs, too. Queen Mary and her brothers, descended on their mother's side from the Duke of Cambridge (a son of King George III), had been the princely Teck family; both brothers took Cambridge as their family name and the elder became the Marquess of Cambridge while the younger was made Earl of Athlone. The two Battenberg princes, Prince Louis and his nephew Prince Alexander, anglicized their family's name to Mountbatten and received the titles of Marquess of Milford Haven and Marquess of Carisbrooke, respectively.

In normal practice, Prince Charles would have been the first sovereign of the house of Mountbatten, but in 1952, Elizabeth II decided her house's name should forever remain Windsor for her successors. She reasoned that it was a felicitous name, deeply associated with the monarchy, and there wasn't a valid reason why it should ever be changed again. Accordingly, in April of that year, two months after her accession, the Queen declared that she and her children would be known as the House and Family of Windsor, and that her descendants, other than female descendants who married and their descendants, would bear the name of Windsor. This probably didn't make Philip very happy, who like most men would have liked to see his name preserved with his descendants (even keeping in mind the irony that the Mountbatten name hadn't come from his father, but from his mother's family).

So, in 1960, after further rumination, the Queen changed her mind and amended her earlier declaration. She now proclaimed that she and her children would continue to be known as the House and Family of Windsor, but her descendants other than those who would be entitled to the title of prince or princess or the children of daughters, would bear the name Mountbatten-Windsor. This made everyone happy, but it will be quite a while before it has any practical effect. The first two generations in the male lines from the Queen or from the Prince of Wales will be princes or princesses, and will not use a last name, but the sons of sons of the Queen's younger sons—not sons of daughters and excepting those with dukedoms—will someday use the last name Mountbatten-Windsor. You may have to read through that again!

A small matter, but one which is presently causing a ruckus of sorts in Scotland, is that of the monarch's postnominal number, the Roman numeral that comes after the king or queen regnant's name. The cause of the Scottish problem goes back to James I of England, who was James VI of Scotland, and his grandson James II of England, who was James VII of Scotland, all because the Union of the Crowns in 1603 didn't do away with the separate identities of the countries. After the thrones were merged in 1707, the succession of the four Georges caused no problem since Scotland had never had a king named George. William IV's postnominal number might have been expected to cause some trouble because Scotland had had a William back in the 13th century, but the Scots didn't have the clout in the 1830s to do anything about it. There was no more difficulty until Queen Elizabeth II came to the throne. The problem is that Scotland never had a Queen Elizabeth I, since England's queen by that name never ruled over the realm of her cousin Mary of Scotland. Therefore, to the Scots—at least the more radical among them—the present queen should be Queen

Elizabeth I in Scotland, or more properly, just Queen Elizabeth, without a postnominal number. This situation is intolerable to the English. Scots nationalism being what it is, it can be safely assumed that England hasn't heard the last of this.

There is another point concerning postnominal numbers. One doesn't have one until there's been another monarch of the same name. For example, Queen Victoria is just that for the time being. If Prince Charles were to have a daughter named Victoria and she were to inherit the throne, then the first Victoria would have to be known as Victoria I and the new one Victoria II. By the by, Prince Charles will in time *probably* be known as King Charles III, although no law prevents him from using another name as king; his grandfather's first name was Albert, not George.

A few more items of royal ritual might stand explanation. Royalty sign themselves with their one name only, except a king or queen, who follow their name with *R*, standing for *Rex* or *Regina*, Latin for king and queen. The Queen Mother retains this *R* after her name. All princes and princesses, including England's royal dukes and their duchesses, sign their one name only. The exception is the Prince of Wales, who follows his name with P (for *Princeps*) if he wishes; the current Prince of Wales does not wish.

One of the most ubiquitous symbols in British life is the royal arms—it appears on passports, government buildings, official documents, and many other places in which it is encountered daily. The royal arms, which is to say the personal arms of Elizabeth II, is also the arms of the United Kingdom as a nation. It has been unaltered since 1837 when Victoria came to the throne and dropped the Hanoverian emblems of her predecessor and uncle, King William IV.

To be precise, the "arms" is the shield-shaped device in the center of what is correctly called the "armorial bearings." One of the difficulties connected with the whole matter of

heraldry is the arcane and colorful language used to describe
its constituent parts. The royal arms is "quartered," that is,
divided into four sections. The four quarters of the Queen's
arms include the emblem of England—three lions—in the
upper-left and lower-right corners, that of Scotland—another
lion—in the upper right, and the harp of Ireland in the lower
left. Surrounding the arms is the Garter, representing England's premier order of knighthood, and inscribed with its
motto, *"honi soit qui mal y pense"*—"evil to him who thinks evil
of it." Surmounting the arms is the crest, a crowned lion
standing on a crown covering a medieval royal helmet. The
"supporters"—creatures, usually animals, which appear to
be supporting or holding the arms—are, in the Queen's case,
a crowned lion on the "dexter" or left side as seen by the
viewer, and a unicorn on the "sinister" or right side as seen
by the viewer. Underneath the whole affair is the royal
motto, *"Dieu et Mon Droit"*—"God and My Right."

Every adult member of the royal family has his or her
own armorial bearings. Those of the Queen's children are
similar to the royal arms. The Prince of Wales's arms sur-
mount the traditional motto of his office, *"Ich Dien"*—old
German for "I Serve." The three-pointed white thing on the
arms that looks like a small freeway overpass is actually a
badge denoting that the bearer is in line of succession to the
throne; the badges of the Queen's other children also have
three pointers; cousins (Gloucesters, Kents) have five pointers. The arms of those not in the line of succession, such as
the Queen Mother and Prince Philip, don't have this device.

A set of rules, drawn up by the Home Secretary (Britain's equivalent of Secretary of the Interior), regulates the
use of arms and associated royal emblems. Whenever some
"Occasion for National Rejoicing" (for example, the Silver
Jubilee) occurs, the law permits the rules to be relaxed so
that the royal symbols can be used on souvenirs, as long as

the manufacturer stays within the bounds of good taste (cans of cat food may *not* be emblazoned with the royal arms), the article is free from any form of advertisement, and it carries no implication of royal usage or approval.

Royal ciphers, or monograms, have been used for centuries to indicate the reign to which a document or coin belongs. That for each sovereign includes the initial, an *R* for king or queen, and postnominal number if there is one. The present Queen uses as her cipher the familiar *EIIR* topped with a stylized Crown of St. Edward. The *"I"* in Victoria's cipher, *VRI*, stood for Imperatrix, Latin for Empress, a dignity borne by English sovereigns from 1876 until 1947 by virtue of their Indian possessions.

Cousins of the Queen who aren't peers are always referred to by their branch, for example, Prince Michael *of Kent*. The wives of these nonducal royal princes use their husbands' names, as for example, Princess Michael of Kent. In Prince Michael's case, his wife couldn't properly call herself "Princess Marie of Kent," that format being reserved for the sisters of such princes (Princess Alexandra of Kent). The present Duke of Gloucester's wife was known as Princess Richard of Gloucester for the short time between her marriage and her father-in-law's death, when she became the new Duchess of Gloucester.

Since the days of Edward VIII's abdication when the subject of morganatic marriage raised its fearsome head, there has been misunderstanding as to what it entails. When a king or prince wishes to marry a woman who for any reason is unable or ineligible to share his official position, morganatic marriage is sometimes resorted to. The origin of the term isn't certain, but most likely it is a corruption of *"more danico,"* marriage "Danish style," referring to the Viking custom which allowed a man to have three wives if he was capable of satisfying all of them. In modern times, it means simply that the wife does not share her husband's position, style or titles and that their children cannot inherit their father's position, style or titles. The marriage is legal, the children are legitimate, and any censure arising from the union is social, not religious. Morganatic marriages are almost extinct in our egalitarian age. The recent marriage of Prince Michael of Kent was not morganatic; since he married a Roman Catholic, he had to renounce his succession rights, but this didn't affect any children of the marriage (as long as they are raised Anglican), nor does it alter his wife's right to share his title.

Finally, there is the subject of titles of the British sovereign's representatives away from Britain. In the semi-autonomous Channel Islands and in the Isle of Man, the Queen's representative is the Lieutenant-Governor. In the member nations of the British Commonwealth which accept Elizabeth II as their Queen, he goes by the title of Governor General, a position now almost always held by a native resident of the country involved, although there is usually talk going around that the Prince of Wales will be made Governor General of one of the larger members of the Commonwealth, such as Canada, or more likely, Australia. The representative in British dependencies is simply titled the Governor. Lieutenant-Governors, Governors General and Governors are all considered to be governing in the place of the absent Queen, and thus are the highest-ranking persons in their individual bailiwicks. (In the major dominions, this is polite fiction, as the Prime Minister is really doing the governing.) The highest title of a representative of the monarch is Viceroy (and Vicereine for his wife), literally the "substitute-king." This was used only in India during the British Raj, when the sovereign himself was titled Emperor of India.

5

Nobility and Honors
EVERYONE LOVES A LORD

The British titled system is unique. Great Britain is the last country with a full-fledged peerage still forming a legislative body and an honors system in which the Crown still confers titles of nobility and knighthoods, doing so on the advice of the government of the day. There are a few countries where already existing titles are recognized by the State—Spain, for example—but only one other, Belgium, still grants them, and then extremely rarely and without the concept of a legislative peerage. In Britain today, there are about 19 peers per million people, a proportion that has actually increased from 14 per million in the Middle Ages.

The terms "nobility" and "aristocracy" are often used interchangeably, but they are not the same thing. Aristocracy, originally meaning government by the "best" class, is now a social concept; nobility, originally meaning "armigerous"—the right to bear one's own arms—is now a legal concept, signifying a granted or inherited status superior to "common" people. The term has come to denote in Britain the five degrees of the peerage—dukes, marquesses, earls, viscounts and barons; the little-understood rank of baronet is a sort of nonpeerage "junior" nobility. On the Continent, a nobleman's precedence was dated from when his arms were first granted (which may have preceded his being created a nobleman), but the English haven't followed this practice, ranking nobles from the date of their "letters patent" (the document officially granting a title of nobility from the sovereign).

The term "peerage" includes only those who actually hold a title of one of the five ranks of nobility (the ecclesiastical peers are a special category), most of whom are eligible to sit in the House of Lords, Britain's upper though far weaker Parliamentary chamber. Wives of peers share their husbands' titles, but are not themselves peeresses in the same sense as peeresses in their own right. A few peerages can be inherited by females if such a provision was specified when the original peerage was created; there are now 18 hereditary peeresses in their own right, as female holders are called. (There are also nearly four dozen "life baronesses" in their own right, which will be explained shortly.) No dukedoms or marquessates can be inherited by a female, but several titles of the lower three ranks may be. (At present, though, there are only countesses and baronesses in their own right.) The earldom of Mountbatten of Burma is inheritable by women, specifically at the late earl's request, whose only issue was two daughters. When the earl was murdered in September 1979, the title passed to his eldest daughter, Patricia, herself the wife of a baron. Her new title, Countess Mountbatten of Burma, outranks that of her husband, the 7th Baron Brabourne. Husbands of peeresses in their own right do not share their wives' styles or titles, although the son, or perhaps daughter, of such a peeress would inherit the title regardless of the father's rank or lack of rank. In the above case, Countess Mountbatten's son, now bearing the courtesy title of Lord Romsey, will someday become the 3rd Earl Mountbatten of Burma (his mother counting as the 2nd earl).

Standing at the top of Britain's noble pecking order is the rank of duke. The ducal title is considered so high in dignity that younger sons of the sovereign upon reaching their majority are created dukes, although their special status outranks that of ordinary dukes. The number of dukes has never been great; today there are only 26, plus the four royal dukes—Edinburgh, Cornwall (his title of Prince of Wales takes precedence over his ducal title), Gloucester and Kent. (The Queen, as Duke of Lancaster, doesn't count.) The ranking (that is, oldest) nonroyal dukedom is held by the Duke of Norfolk, Miles Francis Fitzalan-Howard, called the Earl Marshal. Peers, incidentally, obviously do have first names just like other people, but the last name (for example, Fitzalan-Howard) is the family name used by the peer's relations, not ordinarily by the peer himself. All peers sign themselves simply by their title, such as "Marlborough." (Royal dukes use just their first name—"Philip" or "Edward," for example.)

The style of a duke is "His Grace the Duke of Whatever" (their formal style, rarely used, is Most High, Potent and Noble Prince) and on formal Court occasions the sovereign addresses him as "Our right trusty and right entirely beloved cousin." When you meet a duke (nonroyal), you address him as "Your Grace" (the only peers not addressed as "My Lord"), but you *don't* bow or curtsy to a duke, or to anybody else except members of the royal family. A duke's wife is called a duchess, as one might expect.

Next comes the marquess, pronounced mar-kwess, not mar-kee. Occasionally the French spelling (marquis, though still pronounced mar-kwess) is used in Britain, but it really isn't the done thing, and isn't used in the rolls of the House of Lords. Some Scottish marquesses prefer "marquis" because of its memories of the Auld Alliance with France, Bonnie Prince Charlie, and all that.

A marquess, whose wife is a marchioness (mar-shuness), is also pretty select company, there being only 38 in the whole country. The ranking marquessate is that of Winchester. Their style is "The Most Honorable the Marquess of Whatever" (the formal style being Most Noble and Potent Prince), and are addressed as "My Lord" (rarely "My Lord Marquess" any longer). A marchioness is addressed as "My Lady." The King or Queen calls a marquess "Our right trusty and entirely beloved cousin," just a trifle less grand than the greeting for a duke.

The third ranking title of nobility is earl, which roughly corresponds to the Continental title of count. In fact, an earl's wife is called a countess. ("Earless" would hardly do.) There are today 217 earls, including 5 countesses in their own right. About 40 earldoms do not have "of" in their titles, the reason a technicality having to do with the territorial connection of these titles. The result is that it is often confusing whether an "of" is used or not. For instance, it's Earl Grey, not Earl of Grey, and Earl of Snowdon, not Earl Snowdon. (For the sake of complete accuracy, it should be noted that there are also four marquessates which don't use an "of" either.) The earldom of Crawford and Balcarries is currently the oldest in the United Kingdom. An earl's style is "The Right Honorable, the Earl of Whatever" (earls and below don't have a formal style like dukes and marquesses), and he is addressed as "My Lord" except by the sovereign who ceremonially calls him "Our right trusty and well-beloved cousin."

Next comes the viscount. Only 144 strong, they are numerically more exclusive than the earls. The oldest viscountcy is Hereford. A viscount is styled "The Right Honorable, the Viscount Whatever." They never use "of" in their titles, except for one Scot, the Viscount of Arbuthnot. One calls a viscount "My Lord," except the King or Queen who use "Our right trusty and well-beloved cousin." A viscount's wife is a viscountess.

Finally, at the bottom of the heap, is the baron. There are 531 barons and Scots Lords (see following), 13 baronesses in their own right, 286 life barons, and 44 life baronesses in their own right. Lord Mowbray is the ranking baron. Barons, whose wives are baronesses, are styled "The Right Honorable, the Lord Whatever." (In ordinary usage, all peers from marquesses on down are referred to in newspapers and such as Lord Whatever; only dukes are referred to by their actual titles.) Baronesses in their own right are usually called "Baroness Whatever" rather than "Lady Whatever," which would be the normal female equivalent of Lord; the reason is to distinguish them from mere wives of barons. The sovereign calls a baron "Right trusty and well-beloved," an appreciable drop from the panegyric used for a duke.

There are no barons in the old Scottish peerage (see following for divisions of the peerage); the equivalent rank is Lord of Parliament, abbreviated to Lord. This is not to say that there are no Scottish barons—all creations since 1707 have been made in the peerage of Great Britain or the United Kingdom, with many Scotsmen having been created barons since that time.

In Britain, usage of the title "Baron Whatever" in conversation is limited to foreign barons, such as Baron d'Huart of France. These Continental barons are never referred to as, for example, Lord d'Huart.

The peerage is divided into five classes: those of England, Scotland, Great Britain, Ireland, and the United Kingdom. These divisions tell the story of the three countries making up the United Kingdom. Both England and Scotland had distinct peerages when their two crowns were united in 1603; the distinction lasted, as far as the creation of new titles was concerned, until the Scottish Parliament was merged into that of England's in 1707. At that time, a new peerage, that of Great Britain, was established, and no new distinctly English or Scottish peerages were created. Meanwhile, a separate peerage of Ireland as well as a separate Irish legislature continued until 1801, when it too was merged with the British Parliament; after that date, no more Irish peerages were established. Not all Scottish or Irish peers were automatically entitled to sit in the House of Lords in Westminister. Members of the Scottish peerage had to elect 16 of their number to sit, and the unelected Scots were out of luck unless they also had a new Great Britain or United Kingdom peerage.

After their 1801 union with Great Britain, members of the Irish peerage were permitted to elect 28 of their number to sit in the House of Lords. Since the 1921 establishment of the Irish Free State, no more of these representative Irish peers have been elected; the last, Lord Kilmorey, died in 1961. Of course, Irish peers were often members of the House of Lords by virtue of a Great Britain or United Kingdom peerage, though often a title of lower rank than their old Irish title. To save them embarrassment and even though it complicated the workings of the upper house, they were still addressed by their higher title when sitting in the House of Lords. By the Peerage Act of 1963, all members of the Scottish peerage now sit in the Lords, even though Irish peers without the GB or UK qualification still do not.

It shouldn't in the meantime be assumed that all members of the old Irish peerage were Irish. In some cases an Englishman was granted an Irish peerage because of family ties or associations with that country. The great 18th-century Prime Minister, Pitt, was once asked by his banker, a man named Smith, for the privilege of driving through the Horseguards: "No," said Pitt, "but I can make you an Irish peer." Next day Mr. Smith was Lord Carrington.

One of the more esoteric features of the British system is the matter of courtesy titles. Most peerages, except baronies, have second, and some even third, titles. Some were granted together with the holder's original title to serve specifically as a courtesy title for the heir, and some are accretions from the past—an earl being promoted to a duke, for example, and keeping the earldom in the family. These secondary titles are used by the eldest sons of peers, and are called "courtesy titles." (Viscounts' sons do not use secondary titles as courtesy titles even if their fathers have such titles available.) The holder of a courtesy title is *not* a peer, and is not entitled to a seat in the House of Lords. Courtesy lords can and do run for Commons, which brings about the seemingly odd situation of a sprinkling of earls and viscounts sitting in the lower house. One of the best known of the courtesy titles is the Marquess of Blandford, heir to the Duke of Marlborough. Lord Blandford isn't *really* the Marquess of Blandford, but is only using the title; he inherits the marquessate with the dukedom, but naturally wouldn't himself then use the lower title. His son, in turn, assumes it.

Eldest sons of eldest sons of peers use third titles, if any, of their grandfathers, again on a courtesy basis. In the Marlborough case, the grandson would use the title Earl of Sunderland. In the event a peer doesn't have a secondary title, the offspring just do without. Collateral heirs, such as brothers or nephews, do not use courtesy titles, which are reserved for heirs in the direct line, son or grandson. Nor does a female heir ever use a courtesy title.

This business of courtesy titles is not, incidentally, used by the royal family for its princes, even though the Continental royal houses follow the practice. The late Prince William of Gloucester, to name an instance, when heir to his father the Duke of Gloucester, was known as HRH Prince William of Gloucester, not HRH the Earl of Ulster, his father's second title.

A grace note: Eldest sons of Scottish viscounts and barons are usually titled "The Master of Whatever," such as The Master of Falkland, eldest son of Viscount Falkland.

As has been mentioned, wives of peers, even though they share their husbands' titles, are not themselves peeresses in the same sense as peeresses in their own right; in other words, they are not the holder of the peerage and do not sit in the Lords. They do share their spouses' status as nobles, however. But children, even including eldest sons, are still classified as commoners.

Husbands of peeresses in their own right do not gain noble status from their wives' rank, but an oldest son may use his mother's second title as a courtesy title if she has one, as, for example, the Viscount Reidhaven, son of the Countess of Seafield. Such peeresses sign themselves by their title only as opposed to wives of peers whose legal signature includes their first name and title, such as "Jane Devonshire," wife of the Duke of Devonshire.

A peer's mother is, for example, "the Dowager Duchess of Norfolk" or "the Dowager Lady Londonderry," and his widow, if the dowager is still living, is "Amelia, Duchess of Norfolk" or "Jane, Lady Londonderry," and remains so until she succeeds to the dowagership. (While her husband is still living, a peer's wife is just addressed as the "Duchess of Norfolk" or "Lady Londonderry"—no first name is used.)

Younger sons of dukes are known as, for instance, Lord Randolph Churchill, second son of the Duke of Marlborough, and father of Winston. Children of dukes' second sons have no title at all, unless they earn it themselves, as did Sir Winston. The format for a duke's daughter is Lady Jane Churchill, like her brother using her first name and the family last name (not title of her father). (In many peerages, especially the lower ones, the title and family name are the same.)

A marquess's younger sons and his daughters are styled in the same way as ducal offspring; so are the daughters (but not younger sons) of earls. Women retain this style on marriage (unless marrying a peer of a differing rank), but naturally take their husbands' last names. According to this rule, Princess Anne should correctly be titled "HRH The Princess Anne, Lady Anne Phillips" instead of HRH The Princess Anne, Mrs. Mark Phillips. The reason is that she is a duke's daughter. The same holds true for HRH Princess Alexandra, the Honorable Mrs. Angus Ogilvy, who should be "HRH Princess Alexandra, Lady Alexandra Ogilvy." But these forms would be pretty awkward, and besides, rules very often get "modified" when it comes to the royal family.

Incidentally, the word "Ladyship," so beloved of writers of drawing-room comedies, isn't very much used anymore—generally only by shop clerks and maids.

The format for younger sons of earls is the Honorable John Smith, which puts them in the strange position of being outranked by their sisters. (The same holds true for *all* such sons if no courtesy title is available.) Both the sons *and* daughters of viscounts and barons have the same style as earls' sons, women here also retaining the "Honorable" on marriage, unless they marry peers themselves. Married peeresses in their own right are known as, for example, "The Countess of Seafield (Mrs. Studley Herbert)."

If the daughter of a peer marries a peer of a higher rank, she takes his style and title. But if she marries a peer of a lower rank, she then takes his *lower* style and title. Thus, the daughter of a duke marrying a baron becomes the rank of baroness. The odd situation is that if any of her sisters have married commoners, they retain their ducal daughter's style and title, thereby outranking their sister the baroness.

When a knight—addressed as Sir—is raised to the peerage, he ceases to be called Sir Firstname, and becomes Lord Lastname. Even though the recently ennobled Laurence Olivier technically keeps his knighthood, he is no longer Sir Laurence, but rather Lord Olivier. (Most newly ennobled life barons use their own last name as their title of nobility.)

Into this heady mélange is added another species of peer—the life peer. Although not invented by the Labour Party, life peerages fit nicely with their view of egalitarianism mixed with good old-fashioned British class consciousness. A life peer, now restricted to baronies (about ten new life peerages are created each year), is as much noble as a hereditary peer, and his and his wife's style are identical with hereditary peers, as are his children's styles. The difference is that the peerage itself ceases with the holder's death. Life peerages make a convenient way of honoring preeminent citizens without the necessity of having their descendants sitting in the Lords. But it must be remembered that the honor is not an empty one. The membership in the House of Lords that these peerages confer is still a seat in a functioning legislative chamber, albeit a much-truncated chamber since the turn of this century.

The archbishops and bishops of the 62-million-member Church of England are also peers, the two archbishops, Canterbury and York, ranking between dukes and marquesses, and the 48 bishops between viscounts and barons. Twenty-one of the bishops, according to date of appointment, sit in the House of Lords; the bishops of London, Durham and Winchester sit regardless of their length of tenure. The archbishops, who sign themselves with the Latin names for their sees, *"Cantuar"* and *"Ebor,"* also have permanent seats in the upper house. Archbishops are styled "Most Reverend His Grace Lord Archbishop of ————," and are addressed as "Your Grace." (Bishops are addressed as "My Lord.") Their status as peers ends when they retire, as does that of bishops. The last archbishop, Donald Coggan, who retired in 1980, received a life peerage so that he was able to continue to sit in the Lords.

A number of hereditary peerages have been disclaimed for life, abdicated if you will. This has only been possible since the Peerage Act of 1963, which provided that such renouncements are "irrevocable and operate from the date the instrument of disclaimer is delivered to the Lord Chancellor." When a peerage is given up, by law no other *hereditary* peerage can be conferred, although a new life peerage can be given. (Really almost a moot point today, since only life peerages are still being granted.)

Usually the reason for renouncing a title is political—to permit a high-ranking politician who has inherited a title to retain his seat in the House of Commons. Such was the 2nd Viscount Hailsham's motivation in 1963. As Quintin Hogg, he retained his St. Marylebone seat. In 1970, Mr. Hogg retired from the Commons and was appointed Lord Chancellor. He received the customary life peerage, becoming Lord (Baron) Hailsham of St. Marylebone. (Life peerages cannot be disclaimed, so presumably recipients give the matter serious political thought before accepting them.) This has also happened with Sir Alec Douglas Home, who was 14th Earl of Home before giving up the title to become Prime Minister in 1963. (There is no law that the Prime Minister has to be a commoner, but to effectively lead the country today, he must sit in the Commons; the last Prime Minister to sit in the Lords was the Marquess of Salisbury, who retired in 1902.) Upon his political retirement, he was created Lord (Baron) Home of the Hirsel. Other disclaiming peers include Lord Altrincham, Lord Beaverbrook and Lord Reith, as well as the Viscount Stansgate and the earls of Sandwich and Durham.

It follows that when a peer disclaims his title, his wife loses her title and precedence, too. This must make Christian martyrs out of most such wives. Children of these ex-peers retain their precedence, however, as well as styles and courtesy titles, but they may, if of age, declare they no longer wish to be known by such honorifics. For example, the children of Sir Max Aitken, formerly Lord Beaverbrook, and of Mr. Victor Montagu, once the Earl of Sandwich, have retained their styles of "Honorable." But those of Dr. William Collyer, formerly Lord Monkswell, and Mr. Tony Benn, the one-time Viscount Stansgate (and Mr. Anthony Wedgwood-Benn before he had completed his social metamorphosis), have decided not to use the style.

Sandwiched between the major league of the peerage and the minor league of the knightage is the rank of baronet.

There are currently 1,377 holders of this status, senior of whom is Sir Edmund Bacon, 13th baronet of Redgrave, created in 1611, and junior is Sir Graeme Finlay, 1st baronet of Epping, created in 1964—undoubtedly the last. The baronetage is linked with the peerage in that it is hereditary, but otherwise it is more like a kind of super-knighthood. It has the same five classifications (England, Scotland, and so forth) as the peerage, and four Scottish baronetcies can pass through the female line, having been specially permitted to do so when they were created. Only once has a woman been first created a baronetess—in 1635. There is today only one baronetess on the rolls; she is addressed in the same way as a baronet's wife, but uses "Btss" on documents. Baronets are styled "Sir John Whatever," and the word "Baronet," usually abbreviated to "Bart" or "Bt," is added to their written name. The wife of a baronet is styled "Lady Lastname." Strangely, even though Church of England clergymen who are baronets are styled "Sir," such clerics with knighthoods are not allowed to use the style. It has been estimated by statisticians that the baronetage will disappear through attrition in about 200 years, as the governments since 1964 have ceased creating new baronetcies, and it is unlikely that the practice will be resumed.

Peers still enjoy a number of privileges. Most are well-off financially, and a few are immensely rich (the Duke of Westminster owns vast tracts of London's West End). Other little pleasantries come their way, too. A peer generally finds that reserving a table in a good restaurant is easier for him than for the common herd. Probably less useful to the law-abiding peer is the privilege of exemption from arrest while sitting in the House of Lords. If he does get charged with treason or a felony and goes to trial, he can only be judged by his fellow peers, not by an ordinary court of law. To assault a peer is a crime most British magistrates treat with exceptional severity. But perhaps the most esoteric privilege pertaining to this gilded species was that of being hanged by a silken cord rather than the usual scratchy hemp rope. The last to so avail himself was the Earl of Ferrers, hung in 1760 for murdering his steward. Should the death penalty be reinstituted in Britain, it is possible that some peer may again take advantage of this little refinement.

There are still nobles on the Continent, of course, though very few governments accord the nobility any special status. But that is only to say that most of these Continental aristocrats can't avail themselves of any *official* privileges, such as manning upper houses or being exempt from any of the laws affecting their untitled countrymen. In point of fact, European titles have a tremendous social and economic significance. Snobbery being what it is, corporate directorates and rich hostesses compete quite brazenly for the services of unemployed counts and barons and sundry other bearers of antique inherited rank.

The major factor which separated and made such a vast difference between the British and Continental nobilities was England's use of primogeniture, the principle that the first son inherits both the title and everything that goes with it—the estate, the money and the seat in Parliament. In France, Germany, Russia—all over Europe—the proliferation and consequent cheapening of the nobility was in large part a result of all sons inheriting titles and sharing their fathers' estates. In time, the top-heavy nobility became too big to support. No such thing happened in Britain. Estates were kept intact, the House of Lords stayed manageable, and the younger sons went off to the army, navy, clergy—and sometimes destitution.

Unfortunately for Britain's hereditary nobility, what time hasn't put asunder, the Inland Revenue has. Taxation is doing to the British aristos what the Revolution did to those of France—giving them the axe. It used to be that "death duties" could be circumvented by the simple but probably unnerving expedient of signing over one's property to the heir in advance of one's own expiration. Not now. "Death duties" have been joined by "transfer taxes," crippling what had been a handy method of avoiding the decimation of one's estate.

Except for the sons of the sovereign, the creation of new hereditary peerages in Britain has probably come to an end. The last duke, except royal ones, was created in 1874, the last marquess in 1936. The most recently created hereditary peer was Lord Margadale of Islay, ennobled in 1965. An exception might be peerages granted as a result of royal marriages, such as that of Lord Snowdon, but even here, there aren't any princesses on the horizon who might have a needy husband; Princess Anne's husband will not, it seems, be given a peerage. Baronetcies are no longer granted. Until recently, retiring Lord Mayors of the City of London were given a baronetcy, but no longer.

Life peerages, restricted to baronies, seem to be the last newly created titles of nobility, except for the possible Prime Minister's retirement earldom (Anthony Eden, the Earl of Avon, was the last to exercise this tradition), which would also undoubtedly be a life title. There is the possibility of "titles in abeyance," dormant titles, being revived. For example, in those peerages which cannot be inherited by women (the great majority of the total), a title doesn't become extinct but goes into abeyance if only a daughter or daughters survive the father. If the daughter has a son, he could inherit the title after his mother's lifetime. Two or more daughters of the holder would inherit their father's estate equally, age having no effect on female inheritance rights in the British titled system. If both daughters were then to have a son, neither cousin would inherit the title until the other died. This situation can go on for generations if the cousins have sons, and so on. Some titles have been in abeyance—not extinct—for centuries.

If a collateral relative is to inherit the title, he must be a descendant of the original holder, and not just be related through an antecedent of the original holder. This principle would, as an example, prevent a brother of a first-time holder of a hereditary peerage from inheriting the title. However, the brother or any other collateral relative could inherit a secondary title that goes back to an earlier peer from whom he *is* descended.

In 1925, Parliament passed the Honors (Prevention of Abuses) Act, which made it an offense to accept any money or gifts as an "inducement or reward for procuring titles or honors." Lloyd George's notorious "honors broker," Maundy Gregory, was convicted on this act and sent to prison. What Lloyd George got was £3,000,000 in the Liberal Party's coffers. There are still abuses in the granting of honors, though. Harold Wilson's Resignation Honors List (a tradition with outgoing premiers) ennobled his secretary, Marcia Williams, creating her a life baroness (Lady Falkender), as well as a whole raft of questionably deserving nobles, making a general mockery of the peerage.

For those interested in going deeper into the fantastically intricate subject of the British nobility, there are two great guides to the peerage, *Burke's* and *Debrett's*, now published only at irregular intervals. These enormous tomes list every family member of the titled nobility, as well as the baronetage, knightage and companionage. They also make fascinating reading.

HONORS

Ever since man was running around in loincloths and living in wattle huts, he has wanted some mark of merit or rank or title to set him apart from and above his fellows. This has been especially true of those who have engaged in the profession of arms. Nowhere in the world today is this primitive desire so well served as in the United Kingdom.

Almost all countries still hand out orders and decorations which commend the bearer as worthy of respect from his peers. Some of these honors are genuinely exclusive, such as the American Congressional Medal of Honor and the British Victoria Cross. Some aren't—a third of a million Frenchmen hold the Legion of Honor. But as in so many matters of a ceremonious nature, it is the British who have refined honors to both an art and a science.

Honors in Britain fall into the categories of peerages, baronetages, knightages and companionages. The first two we've already looked at, and seen that they have to a large degree been ossified. But the latter two categories of honors are still being handed out in the thousands.

The British honors system is something that can only be completely understood by the most learned of buffs. Called the "world's most carefully preserved status game," it today includes six remaining orders of knighthood: Garter, Thistle, Bath, St. Michael and St. George, Royal Victorian and British Empire; the Bachelor Knight is a different species. The Queen is personally responsible for appointments to the Garter, Thistle and the Royal Victorian Order; the remainder are in the discretionary power of the government of the day. In addition, there are the nonknightly Order of Merit and Order of Companions of Honor, the first also the Queen's to bestow. Within the Order of the British Empire, only two of the five classes carry the status of knighthood. In the other orders, except the Garter and the Thistle, there is a class called the companionage, which doesn't carry a knighthood either. Many of the lower classes of orders and medals are allocated to government departments, and recipients are decided at the departmental level. The top honors, especially knighthoods themselves, are decided at the highest level—the Prime Minister and the monarch.

The premier order of knighthood in Britain, or in the world for that matter, is the Order of the Garter. Nobody is really certain where its name comes from; the old chestnut about the king stooping over to pick up his dancing companion's dropped garter to the shocked amazement of the other dancers is almost certainly rubbish. But as the motto of the order is "Evil to him who thinks evil of it," the story does lend a romantic note.

Since its inception in 1348 as a reward for skillful jousting, the Garter has been pretty much a preserve of royalty and the high nobility, which is still the case today. (There are never more than two or three dozen members.) One of the extremely few commoners to be a member was Winston Churchill; another is Harold Wilson, knighted in 1976. The Queen is the sovereign of the order, as she is of all British orders of knighthood. The Prince of Wales is an automatic member, according to the order's statutes. The only Lady of the Garter, aside from the Queen, is the Queen Mother, although ex-Queen Juliana is an "Extra Lady," a classification for foreign female sovereigns. Several of the titled knights were high-ranking World War II commanders who had received their peerages for their military exploits. There are also generally a sprinkling of eminent statesmen, such as the Earl of Avon (Anthony Eden). The knights of the Garter have as their chapel St. George's at Windsor. Their cornflower-blue sash is the symbol of the order most often seen on the Queen, extending from left shoulder to right waist, just as the eight-pointed star, which is jeweled for the Queen and Queen Mother, is worn at the left breast.

The Scottish equivalent of the primarily English Garter is the Order of the Thistle, supposedly created in the eighth century. The Thistle, named after the symbol of Scotland, is nearly as exclusively a nobleman's club as is the Garter. Hardly anyone outside of Scotland has ever heard of most of its members. The Thistle sash, like that of the Garter, is worn over the left shoulder. (Sashes of all other orders are worn over the right shoulder.)

The Order of the Bath, formally dated from 1399, unlike the Garter and Thistle, is divided into six divisions: Knights and Dames Grand Cross, military and civil; Knights and Dames Commander, military and civil; and Companions, military and civil. Only Grand Cross and Commander members are titled "Sir" or "Dame." ("Dame" is the female equivalent of a knight and is used as her title; wives of knights are styled "Lady Smith"—but never "Lady Jane Smith," which is the format for peers' daughters.) The Prince of Wales was recently installed as Grand Master. Membership in the Bath is usually reserved for high-ranking officers and civil servants, and is often given as a sort of retirement present. The Bath isn't named after the city, but probably from the ancient ceremonial bathing of knights prior to their dubbing.

The Order of St. Michael and St. George, founded in 1818 by the Prince Regent, is now used to reward British subjects who serve in foreign countries or live in British possessions overseas. It has the same divisions as the Bath.

Next is the Royal Victorian Order, awarded for personal services to the Crown. This is the honor the Queen can bestow on those who have given her long and faithful service or in some other way deserve a personal thanks from their sovereign. It has five classes, the top two carrying a knighthood. The classification awarded is based on the degree of service rendered the sovereign or Crown.

The last order of knighthood is the British Empire. The OBE, now anachronistically misnamed in a time when Britain's imperial status has been diminished nearly to the point of extinction, is the most popular order, at least in the number of awards made. It is waggishly referred to as "Other Bastards' Efforts" since it's often given to retiring civil servants. Of its five classes, only the top two—Knight or Dame

Grand Cross and Knight or Dame Commander—carry a knighthood and the title of Sir or Dame. The Commanders, Officers and Members don't get a title, which makes for all sorts of errors in American newspapers. Much of the U.S. press had the Beatles mistakenly listed as "Sir Ringo," etcetera, after they were awarded MBEs.

One additional type of knight sometimes pops up, the Knight Bachelor. These aren't knights of a specific order, they're just knights. The classification is little used today (Knights Bachelor aren't regarded as the equal of knights of the orders, at least not by those who know about these sorts of things), but is sometimes necessary in the arcane world of British honors: Before a person can be invested as knight of any of the orders, he is first dubbed a Knight Bachelor by the Queen—later, the new knights are invested at installation ceremonies of the individual orders.

Two other orders, nonknightly, are available to honorworthy Britons. The Order of Merit has no rank or title, but is very much coveted. Its membership (limited to 26 at any one time) has included many of the most distinguished persons in Britain, men and women of tremendous achievement, such as T. S. Eliot, Lord Russell, Graham Sutherland and Henry Moore. The Queen awards the OM at her personal choice. The Order of Companions of Honor is something like a junior Order of Merit, with emphasis on political and governmental service.

A final point on knighthoods: what the Queen gives, the Queen can take away. Twice in modern British history have knights been stripped of the accolade—"formal degradation," it's called. The first was the Irish patriot, Sir Roger Casement, KCMG (Knight Commander of the Order of St. Michael and St. George), deknighted in 1916 for treason and then hanged. Late in 1979, Sir Anthony Blunt, KCVO (Knight Commander of the Royal Victorian Order) and former Keeper of the Queen's Pictures, had his knighthood rescinded for the same offense, albeit an offense which his government covered up for more than two decades and for which he was never tried. Supposedly granted immunity in the 1950s for turning state's evidence in the Philby-Burgess-Maclean spy scandal, his part in the affair was finally brought to light in 1979, and because of the resulting furor in the press, the Queen had no choice but to take away his knighthood. At that, the Queen's knowledge of the cover-up was questioned, the assumption being that she must have been aware (or *should* have been aware) of Blunt's past when he joined the royal Household. At least, Mr. Blunt didn't receive the treatment accorded to degraded knights in medieval days, when their swords were broken over their heads, the stub then used to chop it off!

On about 14 occasions each year, a great crush of automobiles backs up on the Mall, all heading straight for Buckingham Palace where the Queen awaits, sword at the ready, prepared to hold another semiannual investiture. Most of the recipients have been announced in the New Year's and Birthday (her's, not their's) honors lists. The recipients, almost all with their allotted two guests in the audience, are lined up according to the grade they're about to receive. On cue, each solemnly marches up to the Queen, who either dubs the luckier ones as knights or dames, or pins medals on the great majority who are receiving the lesser honors. The Queen doesn't actually say anything on the lines of "I dub thee Sir Such and Such" or "Arise, Dame This or That." She merely taps the new knight or dame first on the right, then on the left, shoulder. All receive a word or two of greeting from their monarch; aides are stationed close by to shunt off those who become overly talkative or, more likely, are frozen with fear. Most of those newly honored will treasure every second of the occasion for the rest of their lives.

Another "honor," but of an entirely different sort, is the use of the legend "By Royal Appointment." The familiar coat of arms underscored with the words "By Appointment to Her Majesty the Queen"—or to other members of the royal family—appears on many different products and in the windows of shops dealing in services as well as supplies to the royal Household. If a manufacturer produces several different things, only those enjoying the royal family's "custom" are thus "appointed" and can be advertised as such. The placards over the shop entrances always specify what it is the appointment applies to—soup canners, kilt makers, crown jewelers, and so on. Tradesmen have recently been able to be appointed suppliers to Prince Charles, who joins his mother, father and grandmother in this exclusive clique. Many shops still display arms and appointments to former kings and queens. Not all items which have a royal warrant are actually used by that particular member of the royal family. For example, although Benson and Hedges supplies cigarettes "By Appointment," they are for the benefit of guests in the palaces.

Contrary to popular notion, royal warrant holders don't supply their goods and services free. The Queen pays up like everyone else. But there is no question that the warrant gives the holder great prestige as well as valuable economic advantage. Royal warrants are administered through the Lord Chamberlain's office, and to get one the firm is required to have supplied one of the royal households for at least three years. The Queen personally reviews all successful warrant applications before they are granted, and then every 10 years thereafter the warrant is again reviewed. A warrant given in the name of a particular member of the royal family is still valid for 10 years after the grantor's death, but the arms must be amended "to the late . . ." The 1,000 or so warrant holders naturally have a "Royal Warrant Holders Association" to guard against the perfidious attempts by certain German,

Japanese and American firms to fraudulently imply royal favor by using the royal arms in their advertising.

There is one last concept closely associated with all the foregoing pomp: precedence. Every government in the world has an intricately drawn up table of precedence—a list setting out the exact order of the most important members of society, by title or position. As would be expected, the sovereign heads the table of precedence in a kingdom, just as the president heads a republic's list. At the bottom of Britain's table of precedence are two ranks—Esquire and Gentleman—which would appear to be thoughtfully included for people who don't otherwise place. But such is not the case; both have a legal meaning, and one which does not include just anybody. Even though mail-order salesmanship has corrupted the title of esquire, there are still rules which formally govern its use. For example, eldest sons of noblemens' younger sons are officially esquires, as are the sons of baronets and knights; commanders, companions and non-knightly members of any order of knighthood, as well as barristers and justices of the peace, are also esquires. There is a long list of additional offices which carry the title, but the point to be made is that by no means is everybody *legally* entitled to the use of the title of esquire.

At the bottom of the table of precedence is the category of Gentleman. This title is so popularized as to have become meaningless. But again, only certain persons are entitled legally to the use of the word: solicitors for instance. Technically the category of Gentlemen includes any man with a legal coat of arms, which, after all, is the original definition of nobility. But it isn't likely that any eligible person will sign their name followed by the appellation "Gent."

6

Ornaments
FIT FOR A QUEEN

Throughout the history of man, vanity has played a large part in his foible-studded story. To mark that vanity, jewelry became the most highly visible badge. It is hard to think of jewels as anything other than a luxury—simply body ornaments, pleasing to senses of sight and feel—and ego. But to royalty, jewels, fashioned into every kind of embellishment from crowns to stomachers to shoe clips, have proven as necessary to the maintenance of their status as have food and drink to the sustenance of their bodies. And there is nowhere else on earth another accumulation of great jewelry as that which adorns the British royal family.

The keystone of this treasure is the portion owned by the State—the great Crown Jewels. The Regalia—that part of the Crown Jewels used in the coronation ceremony—are seen by more than a million people each year in the Jewel House of the Tower of London. Their monetary value—virtually incalculable—is relatively unimportant; to the British nation, they are priceless. The original Regalia that was used by monarchs up to Charles I was dismantled during the Commonwealth, the gold melted down for coinage and the jewels sold. Only the ampulla, anointing spoon, and Queen

Elizabeth I's saltcellar were saved. When the monarchy was restored, new Regalia were made for the coronation of Charles II in 1661. These are essentially the jewels on display today, with the addition of new crowns.

If any crown can be described as the Crown of England, it is that of St. Edward. Made for the coronation of Charles II, this was a copy of the crown probably originally worn by Edward the Confessor, and perhaps even earlier by Alfred the Great. It has been worn at all but three coronations since that of Charles II. Fashioned entirely of gold and set with precious and semiprecious stones, its two crossed arches are depressed in the center and topped with a gold ball and cross.

This crown, despite its historic value, doesn't have nearly the monetary value of the others in the Regalia; none of the stones is in itself famous or historic. It weighs about five pounds, much too heavy to be worn for any protracted period. Inside the crown is a velvet cap, called a "Cap of Estate." Henry VII first started wearing a crown over such a liner, presumably for greater comfort, and later all crowns worn by royalty and nobles on State occasions were set on a Cap of Estate. St. Edward's Crown is worn only once during a reign—at the coronation of the monarch. The point in the ceremony when the Archbishop of Canterbury sets the crown on the sovereign's head is the actual moment of coronation. It is worn for only a short while before being exchanged for the lighter Imperial State Crown, Britain's real "workaday" crown.

The headdress which the Queen wears once each year at the State opening of Parliament is this magnificent Imperial State Crown, the most valuable piece of jewelry in the world. It was made in 1838 for the coronation of Queen Victoria, and has since been the most used of Britain's crowns. When the Cullinan diamond, the largest ever discovered, was found in 1905, it was presented to King Edward VII as a birthday present by the government of South Africa. He had it cut into four large stones as well as a number of smaller ones. The main stones are called the four Stars of Africa. The second Star, an oblong weighing 317 carats, is set in the front of the band of the Imperial State Crown, just above the edging of ermine.

Above the row of pearls is the most historic jewel in the crown (for that fact, the most historic in the entire collection), the Black Prince's ruby, which was worn by Henry V at the Battle of Agincourt. This stone has taken pride of place in the State crowns of 20 generations of British sovereigns. The ruby is set in the front of the four crosses pattée (an ancient form of cross) which alternate with four fleurs-de-lys around the band. Inset in the top of the huge ruby is another, much smaller ruby, of a slightly different hue. The Black Prince's ruby was struck with a sword blow, and the small stone was used to "repair" the damage.

Two solidly diamond-encrusted arches cross each other, and from their intersection hang four drop pearls (which, like the Black Prince's ruby, were fortunately not lost during the Commonwealth), reputedly the earrings of Queen Elizabeth I. There is a diamond-studded sphere above the arches which is surmounted by another diamond-covered cross pattée. In the center of this top cross is St. Edward's sapphire, said to have been worn in the ring of the canonized king, Edward the Confessor. Apart from these stones, the crown contains five rubies, 11 emeralds, 18 sapphires, 277 pearls, and 2,783 diamonds. It has an internal fitting like that of a Guards officer's bearskin, and is carefully adjusted for each new monarch to take the crown's two-and-a-half-pound weight evenly on the head. Because of this weight, the Queen used to wear it for several hours around the palace before opening Parliament each year to get accustomed to it. After 28 years, she no longer needs to do so.

The Imperial State Crown is used one more time in each reign—to rest atop the coffin, with the King's Orb and Royal Scepter, until the monarch is interred at Windsor.

Besides these two central crowns in the Regalia, there are several others which are now used extremely rarely or not at all. The crown made for Queen Elizabeth The Queen Mother's coronation as Queen Consort in 1937 is of particular value since it contains the world-famous Koh-i-noor diamond. The word means "mountain of light," and from its setting in the cross pattée over the headband, it resembles the headlight on a miner's helmet. The 108-carat stone was given to Queen Victoria, who used it as a brooch or bracelet, but it was later mounted in the crowns of Queen Alexandra, Queen Mary, and finally Queen Elizabeth.

Queen Mary's crown is similar to Queen Elizabeth's, but more graceful, with four (rather than two) much more flowingly curved arches rising to its orb and cross pattée. The third and fourth Stars of the Cullinan diamond, known as the Lesser Stars and technically not a part of the Crown Jewels, were originally set in this crown, but are now in the personal possession of the Queen, having been given to her by her grandmother. The larger of the two is 92 carats, and it was in the cross pattée on the top the crown's orb; the smaller, 62 carats, was in the center of the headband. The two stones were set so as to be detachable and worn as a brooch, something the present queen occasionally does—she refers to them as "Granny's Chips." This crown also originally held the Koh-i-noor diamond, now in Queen Elizabeth's crown, and was replaced, like the Cullinan Stars, with paste. Either of these crowns could be worn by a Queen Consort of King Charles III at his coronation; the major gems are still interchangeable.

The Imperial Crown of India was made for the Durbar in Delhi in 1911. Since the Imperial State Crown could not be taken out of England, George V had to have something to wear. So this crown, which closely resembles that of Queen Mary, was made for the occasion. It contains over 6,000 diamonds and will probably never be worn again.

Although it is not in the nature of crowns, as opposed to tiaras and diadems, to be really attractive head ornaments, there is one which serves the function of deliberate majesty and is as well a lovely piece of jewelry. The small diamond crown of Queen Victoria is in heraldic Tudor form, and was made in 1877 at the Queen's own expense because she found the Imperial State Crown too heavy. It is often seen in the later pictures and the coinage of Victoria's reign, on the Queen's head over a lace mantel. It was designed to be worn sitting on top of the head rather than fitting over it, the latter being the normal course.

The ugliest crown of the lot is the latest, that made for Prince Charles at his investiture as Prince of Wales in 1969. It is made of solid gold, with 75 diamonds and 12 emeralds. The general effect can best be dismissed as unfortunate.

After St. Edward's Crown and the Imperial State Crown, the next most important piece of the Regalia is the Royal Scepter. As with all the Regalia except the Imperial State Crown, the scepter is used by the sovereign only once during a reign—at the coronation. It was altered during Edward VII's reign so that it now holds the largest cut diamond in the world, the Cullinan's first Star. This egg-sized rock weighs 530 carats—nearly four ounces—and is detachable from the clever prong device holding it in place, a feature that ingeniously allows it to be worn as a brooch or pendant. Above the diamond is a huge amethyst surmounted by a diamond-encrusted cross with an emerald in its center. The staff is gold, with a diamond-pavé handle.

The ampulla and anointing spoon are the only certain complete relics of pre-Cromwellian days. Both are made of pure gold, the former to hold the holy oil used to anoint the sovereign and the latter to pour the oil into. The ampulla is shaped like an eagle. The head unscrews to admit the oil, which then flows out of the beak.

The King's Orb symbolizes the "worldwide domination" of Christianity. It is a hollow globe of gold encircled by a pearl-edged band set with rubies, sapphires, diamonds and emeralds. The most prominent stone is a large amethyst set under the cross.

The remaining Regalia includes the several State swords, the coronation rings, the spurs (not worn by a queen regnant, but merely touched by her during the service), and the bracelets, or armills.

The personal jewelry collection of the Queen of England even beggars the Crown Jewels. It is without question the greatest private collection in the world, and because of its many historical associations, is almost literally beyond ordinary measures of worth. The bulk of it has been handed down to her by former English queens, Victoria, Alexandra, Mary and the present Queen Mother. The collection comprises resplendent tiaras and diadems, necklaces and bracelets and earrings fashioned of robin's-egg-sized diamonds, many strings of splendidly matched and graduated pearls, countless brooches, each worth a queen's ransom. There is some question whether the jewels are inalienable from her position; the part of the collection technically classified as Crown Jewels (State property) was automatically vested in her person on the day of her accession. But it is a fact that her jewelry was bequeathed to her as the future queen rather than as private gifts to a daughter or granddaughter. The bulk of the still enormous collection of the Queen Mother (including her favorite tiara and the one in which she has been for many years most often photographed wearing, the fabulous Honeycomb Tiara, as well as another Russian-fringe-style tiara which she loaned to both the Queen and Princess Anne to wear as brides) will someday go to the Queen. The jewels that have been and will be given to Princess Margaret are but a tiny fraction compared to those of Elizabeth.

A description of some of the more important pieces of the Queen's collection provides a fascinating glimpse into the jeweled riches of Britain's reigning family.

Tiaras are not crowns, but serve almost the same function for the Queen. The unique sumptuousness of her tiaras instantly signals her unmistakably royal station. It is difficult to imagine anyone other than a member of royalty wearing them; they weren't designed as mere jewelry, but as badges of rank to help focus the limelight always shining down on the monarch. Such attention is always concentrated to a greater extent on a regnant queen than on a king, especially if she is gloriously bejeweled. Nobody cares what a king is wearing. Among the 20 or so tiaras that the Queen owns, there are three or four particularly magnificent ones which she wears most often and have become world-famous ornaments which serve to enhance the majesty of her office as well as to grace her person.

Probably the most outstanding among them is one of 15 interlocking circles of diamonds, threaded with swags of smaller diamonds. In the center of each of the circles can be hung either enormous teardrop-shaped pearls or teardrop-shaped cabochon (a very old type of cut, meaning smooth or without facets) emeralds. When the tiara is hung with the pearls, the Queen usually wears a dazzling pearl-and-diamond necklace called the Jubilee Necklace, given to Queen Victoria for her first Jubilee. Its centerpiece is topped with a crown and a large teardrop-shaped pearl hangs from the center diamond-and-pearl "quatre-foil." When the emeralds are suspended in the diamond loops of the tiara, the Queen wears a cabochon emerald necklace and earring set, the necklace with huge drop diamonds complementing the emeralds.

The tiara known as "Granny's Tiara" is said to be the Queen's favorite, being the first one she owned, a wedding present from her grandmother. It had been a gift to Queen

Mary from the "Girls of Great Britain and Ireland," and is a spiked and crenellated affair solidly studded with diamonds, none small. The Queen has had a band of diamonds added to the base of this piece, presumably so that it will appear higher on her hairdo and thus be more visible.

The tiara worn at the White House State Dinner during the Bicentennial visit is called the Russian Fringe, or Sunray, and originally belonged to Queen Alexandra. It is a graduated bank of platinum rays, each solid with diamonds. The shape, that of an old Russian peasant headdress, was a style affected by the ladies of the Russian court.

The Diamond Diadem, a part of the Crown Jewels, is worn by the Queen to and from Parliament for the annual State opening (the Imperial State Crown is worn while she reads the speech from the throne). It was also worn by the Queen on the way to her coronation. This beautiful piece was made for George IV's coronation, but has never been worn by a man since. It is a circlet of diamonds and pearls topped with four crosses pattée alternating with four floral sprays of roses, shamrocks and thistles, all covered with diamonds. The diadem is familiar as the headdress worn by the Queen on Britain's postage and currency.

As indispensable to the Queen as her handbag and gloves are her famous pearls. Most of the strings were gifts from her parents and grandparents. All are supremely beautiful and lustrous single-, double- and triple-strand sets of perfectly colored and graduated natural pearls, with clasps fashioned from large diamonds. They are worn habitually by the Queen, but only during the day; nights are reserved for diamonds and other stones.

A form of jewelry unique to female royalty are the "Family Orders." In Britain, these date back to King George IV who instituted his own order in 1820; they have been a feature of every reign since except that of Edward VIII. The orders are small oval cameos of the sovereign, hand-painted on ivory, and surrounded by diamonds and other jewels, the whole attached to pastel moiré ribbons and pinned to the top left side of the bodice on formal evening occasions, and meant simply as jewelry peculiar to royalty. They are absolutely first-rate works of art, made with great technical skill. The Queen wears two orders, those of her grandfather and father. The cameos, which were painted by Hay Wrightson, show the two kings in uniforms of Admiral of the Fleet, the paintings circled in diamonds and topped with imperial crowns. The royal ciphers, worked in small diamonds, are on the reverse sides, surely the only of her jewels meant never to be seen. The order for George V is on a sky-blue ribbon, that for George VI on a rose-pink ribbon. Elizabeth II's own order shows her head and shoulders in evening dress, wearing the diamonds which were a wedding present from the Nizam of Hyderabad. The order is on a watered-silk chartreuse yellow ribbon, and is worn by the Queen Mother, Princesses Anne, Margaret, and Alexandra, the Duchesses of Kent and Gloucester, the Dowager Duchess of Gloucester, and Princess Michael of Kent.

Rounding out the jewelry worn by the Queen are the stars of the various orders of knighthood, of all of which she is sovereign. The single star which she customarily wears is that of the Garter, hers being a diamond-encrusted model. Other stars, also jeweled, are worn when attending services for particular orders or on occasions pertinent to the other orders. On State visits at home and abroad, monarchs wear each other's decorations, which explains some of the oddly shaped and colored badges and ribbons seen on the Queen when photographed with foreign royalty.

7

Occasions of State
PRECISION PAGEANTRY

Though the function of monarchy is to legitimize and personify the State, its real appeal lies in the fact that it usually provides a good show, creating an interest and loyalty no other form of government can hope to match. The panoply of great figures, hereditarily and legally set above all others in their kingdom, treated with massive deference and kept in luxury, has proven immensely durable in Great Britain—and will without doubt continue as long as the central figures' only power is to head society and serve as its symbol, leaving the governing to those elected to do so.

Of all royal pageantry, the greatest show—the superspectacle of monarchy—is a coronation. One of the things that make coronations so appealing is their rarity. Only the British carry on with this religious ceremony-cum-Super Bowl. The Continental monarchies have abandoned it as anachronistic, unnecessary, and far too expensive. But in the United Kingdom, it is a momentous occasion, one of those royal extravaganzas the British still carry off incomparably well.

There have been four coronations in Britain so far in the 20th century: those of King Edward VII in 1902, King

George V in 1911, King George VI in 1937, and Queen Elizabeth II in 1953. Edward VIII wasn't king long enough for his coronation planned for 1937. This was surely a blessing for Britain; a *crowned* king's abdication would have been all that much more traumatic a blow to the throne. Chances are good that there won't be another coronation until the 21st century. The present Queen will in the year 2000 reach her 74th birthday, no age at all for this remarkably healthy and robust woman. Her eldest son will be 52 in the same year, which is, incidentally, seven years younger than Edward VII when he came to the throne.

Elizabeth II succeeded her father on February 6, 1952, though she wasn't crowned until June 2 of the following year. The long interval may seem immoderate, but it should be kept in mind that the royal family required an appropriate mourning period, and then the seasonal timing had to be considered in the light of the enormous tourist attraction of a coronation. Therefore, the June day in 1953 was chosen, with the (hoped for) likelihood of pleasant weather.

Naturally, it was raining, cold and miserable on the appointed day. Nevertheless, the streets of London had been filled since the previous evening with millions of spectators, cramming every possible niche and vantage point along the procession route. The gray skies lifted a bit with the news that an Englishman, Edmund Hillary (soon to be knighted), had just been the first man to climb Mount Everest, the world's highest peak. This was taken as some sort of heaven-sent sign that a second "Elizabethan Age" had begun, which today sounds like pure hyperbole, but was regarded seriously a quarter century ago when Britain was just beginning to lift itself out of the economic defeat of its World War II victory. In fact, the still-operating Rationing Board generously allotted each Briton an extra pound of sugar and quarter pound of margarine that coronation week.

The coronation was stage-managed by the Duke of Norfolk, Earl Marshal and premier duke of England (and

Chief Butler, too, for that matter), Bernard Marmaduke Fitz-alan-Howard. He had had good practice, serving in the same capacity for the coronation of the Queen's father 16 years earlier.

One of the contretemps he resolved was finding some of the precious anointing oil, the last vial of which was lost when the Westminster deanery was bombed during the War. After some masterly Sherlock Holmesian detective work, he tracked down four ounces of the original base oil for the prescription for the ointment in the possession of one Mr. M. B. Mavrogordato, a resident of the village of Lingfield, in Surrey. It was consecrated anew, and the Queen was thus anointed properly.

Another potentially sticky situation concerned the nation's former king, the Duke of Windsor. His niece invited *him* to the ceremony, but the invitation didn't include his duchess. Uncle David therefore petulantly refused to go, instead watching the coronation on a TV set in a friend's Paris mansion.

The Queen left Buckingham Palace that Wednesday morning dressed in what can only be described as glittering raiment. Her gown was designed by Norman Hartnell, the Bond Street couturier who had been designing clothes for ladies of the royal family for years. It was done in white satin, cut fairly simply but embroidered in a marvelous array of precious and semiprecious stones in designs representing the Commonwealth—the rose of England, thistle of Scotland, leek of Wales, shamrock of Ireland, wattle of Australia, and maple leaf of Canada. The Diamond Diadem was on her head, and a single-strand choker of jelly bean-sized diamonds at her throat, a necklace which Queen Victoria had had made and which had been worn by every queen on her coronation day since. She was wearing the long crimson Robe of State, embellished with gold lace and lined and edged with ermine, held together at the front with the chain of the Order of the

Garter. The Duke of Edinburgh, dressed in the uniform of an Admiral of the Fleet, was at her side.

The Duke's role had been dicey from the start. Since England has no rubric for consorts, his part had to be played more or less by ear. He couldn't even hark back to Prince Albert as a role model, since Victoria had married Albert after her coronation. Some members of the Coronation Executive Committee felt he should ride beside or behind the State Coach on horseback, or even in a separate coach. But the Queen would have none of it, and decreed that his place would be with her in the State Coach, and that furthermore he would be the first to make obeisance to her after the crowning. The Queen had also earlier made him chairman of the Coronation Commission, the body which decided the broader questions of principle concerning the conduct of the entire coronation, so at least he hadn't been odd man out during the planning.

When the Queen and Duke arrived at the Abbey at 11:25 A.M., the scene of English coronations since the 13th century, they pulled up under the canopy of the Annexe, a sort of elaborate lean-to constructed against the entrance to the church. One of these temporary but expensive structures had been built for each coronation since William IV. Its purpose was to provide a place to marshal, or line up, the procession before going into the Abbey proper. It also served the happy secondary function of providing a loo for the Queen and a place for the leading players to down a quick sandwich.

The coronation ceremony itself is essentially religious in nature. For all its splendor and solemnity, the ritual is simple and full of meaning. There are several main elements in the service. First is the recognition, in which the Queen was "presented" to the people in the Abbey. It is the symbolic way that the English assert that their monarch does not make herself sovereign, as have czars and other assorted despots throughout history, but that she is queen through the recognition of her people. She then solemnly swore to govern according to the established laws of the kingdom.

Next came the anointing, the trickiest part of the service, and during which the television and movie-news cameras were discreetly turned away. A gold canopy, held up by four Garter knights, was placed over the Queen to shield her divestiture, a necessary preparation for the anointing. The six Maids of Honor who had held her train during the procession into the Abbey now lifted off all her jewelry and robes, piece by piece, earrings excepted. A relatively simple white pleated linen gown was put on over her satin coronation dress. Understandably, all this had to be done quite gingerly and gracefully so as not to allow even a hint of embarrassment to the principal.

The Archbishop of Canterbury (Geoffrey Fisher in 1953), chief prelate at the ceremony (and the cranky old curmudgeon who had tried unsuccessfully to bar television cameras from the Abbey), then dipped his thumb into some of the oil from the ampulla which had been poured into the spoon, and daubed the Queen on her hands, breast and head with the sign of the Cross. From a religious standpoint, this was the central and most meaningful part of the two-and-a-half-hour-long service—the crowning itself more the secular affirmation of Elizabeth's sovereignty.

The cameras were now turned back on, and the Queen was re-robed with an incredibly resplendent and varied series of garments. The Dean of Westminster and the Mistress of the Robes carried out with dignity this somewhat harrowing task of publicly re-dressing the Queen with half the world watching. When all the robes and ornaments were in place, she was given the Royal Scepter for one hand and the Rod with Dove (another scepter) for the other. Then came what is surely the supreme moment of a sovereign's life, the crowning by the Archbishop of Canterbury with St. Edward's Crown, the ultimate symbol of monarchy in the kingdom. At this same instant when the crown was being lowered onto the Queen's head, every peer and peeress in the Abbey put on the gold coronets of their rank with a great sweep of upraised ermined arms, looking like nothing so much, according to one witness, as a "great gaggle of swans."

An important point should be made about this part of the coronation. Elizabeth was crowned "Queen of England" *only*, not of Great Britain nor of the United Kingdom nor of the Commonwealth. The reason was that the coronation is a ceremony of the Church of England, and only in England is this denomination the "established" church.

Everything after the crowning was anticlimax. Immediately following the supreme act, she was moved from King Edward's Throne to the Coronation Chair, where she received the homage of her husband who recited the words, "I, Philip, Duke of Edinburgh, do become your liege man of life and limb, and of earthly worship; and faith and truth I will bear unto you, to live and die, against all manner of folks. So help me God." He followed the archaic profession with a peck on his wife's cheek. The dukes of Gloucester and Kent then did substantially the same thing, and were in turn succeeded by the senior member of each of the five ranks of the nobility—who didn't get to give the Queen a kiss.

At this point in the coronation of a king, the queen consort would be crowned, not technically by constitutional right, but rather at the bidding of the king. A queen consort does not in any sense become a co-sovereign, but remains her husband's subject. She has her chair on the throne platform next to the king's, only two steps lower. Prince Philip had no such thing; his chair was off next to the Duke of Gloucester. (The throne platform, in fact, the whole transept of the Abbey as well as the royal family's gallery, was specially and temporarily constructed just for the coronation. Most of the church that morning was covered with red carpets which were taken up after the service. Visitors to Westminster Abbey today get little feeling of the building as it appeared on Coronation Day.)

Next, the Queen received communion, and for this the Duke of Edinburgh joined her as an equal partner. For the sacrament, the rich gold robes and St. Edward's Crown were removed, never again to be worn in her reign.

Finally, the Queen was draped in the Imperial Robe of royal purple, edged with ermine, beautifully embroidered in gold, and also destined never to be worn again by this sovereign. With the Imperial State Crown on her head, the Orb in her left hand and the Royal Scepter in her right, it was 1:50 when she proceeded out of the Abbey to begin the long roundabout drive through London back to the palace.

The ride back was in the same State Coach which was used for the shorter journey to the Abbey that morning. The coach was cleverly fitted with special holders in which to place the Orb and Scepter to give the illusion the Queen was holding them. There were 20 other coaches and carriages in the procession, as well as 550 horses (down from the 6,000 horses in George V's coronation procession). The morning drizzle turned to a downpour all through the afternoon, and the powdered (actually cornstarched and floured) wigs of the grooms turned to soggy dumplings by the time the procession turned into the forecourt of Buckingham Palace. The Queen and Duke appeared many times on the balcony throughout the evening, each appearance generating an enormous roar from the hundreds of thousands of people jamming the entire length of the Mall.

The nobility naturally had had a central place in all these proceedings, although since there wasn't enough room for all of them in the Abbey, they were made to ballot for the available seats. For the service, they had to wear a prescribed costume, dictated by tradition and enforced by the Earl Marshal. Veteran observers of Britain's upper classes could as easily distinguish between the various ranks as tell the difference between a sergeant and a corporal: the coronets for dukes and duchesses were gold circlets with eight strawberry leaves on the rim and their coronation robes had four rows of ermine tails around the perimeter; silver gilt coronets with four strawberry leaves alternating with four silver balls on points for marquesses and marchionesses and three and a half rows of ermine tails on their robes; eight raised silver balls alternating with eight strawberry leaves, and three ermine tail rows for earls and countesses; 16 raised silver balls and two and a half rows of tails for viscounts and viscountesses; and finally six silver balls and two rows for barons and baronesses. The Prime Minister, Sir Winston Churchill, wasn't a peer and thus didn't rate a coronet, but was resplendent nevertheless in his gorgeous costume as Lord Warden of the Cinque Ports.

Many of the peers couldn't easily afford these costumes. It was rumored that a petition was sent to the Queen that they be allowed to attend in civvies, but seated apart—in effect, a "Pen for Poor Peers." ("Quite untrue," said the Earl Marshal.)

The coronation remains the most significant event in which the monarch and the people are drawn together in sort of an imaginative act of unity. Its rarity assures each coronation a large place in history.

Just as rare have been the great jubilees celebrating anniversaries of monarchs' accessions. Jubilees are a fairly recent phenomenon in Britain. There had been a halfhearted jubilee for George III in 1809, really a political maneuver to prop up the incapacitated throne, but it didn't amount to much and it doesn't rank with the organized sorts of national celebration the later jubilees became. The first real one was Queen Victoria's Jubilee of 1887 celebrating her 50 years of monarchy; although preceded by 13 English sovereigns who had reigned for at least 25 years, she was the first to have an organized jubilee to mark an anniversary of her reign.

If the idea of a Silver (25th) Jubilee had occurred to Victoria, it would surely have been canceled because of the death of Prince Albert in the 24th year of her reign. The Queen's Jubilee in 1887 (which was not actually called a "Golden Jubilee," although it is now often referred to as such) was primarily a British celebration, as compared with the Diamond (60th) Jubilee held 10 years later in which the glory of her vastly expanded empire was marked with an extravaganza of imperial lavishness. The old Queen was frail enough during the first jubilee, and by the time of the second celebration was nearly infirm. But still she was the focal point of a great part of the world by 1897, her self-imposed isolation having been completely forgiven, the recipient of unbelievable loyalty and respect from her subjects on every continent.

There was a 38-year gap before the next jubilee—a silver one to mark George V's 25 years on the throne in May of 1935. The young princesses of York, Elizabeth and Margaret, attended the Thanksgiving Service at St. Paul's Cathedral with their parents, who themselves would be king and queen a year and a half later. One of the most fascinating photographs of the Jubilee and of the era shows the girls in their matching pink-colored coats, with their mother, the future Queen Elizabeth, looking her usual furbelowed and overfrilled self, and their aunt, the Duchess of Kent, the very image of drop-dead thirties chic.

King George VI didn't live long enough to celebrate a Silver Jubilee; the next one was held for Queen Elizabeth II in 1977. Britain went all out to make the celebration nearly as momentous as that for her coronation 24 years earlier, and the country experienced a great gush of royalist feelings. The Prince of Wales headed the Jubilee Commission, resigning from the navy to do so. Naturally, the major events were planned for late spring, the height of London's tourist sea-son. Fortunately for the prestige of the Crown and the pound sterling, the whole show was a smashing success.

The highlight of the months-long series of Jubilee events was the service of Thanksgiving in St. Paul's on June 7, Jubilee Day itself. For the first time since her coronation and the second time in her reign, the Queen and Prince Philip rode out of Buckingham Palace in the Royal State Coach, the fairy-tale vehicle gilded all around with carved crowns and crests and wonderful 18th-century painted panels, the whole pulled by eight magnificent Windsor grays. It traveled down London's ceremonial axis, the Mall, and continued under Admiralty Arch into the Strand and Fleet Street, up Ludgate Hill, finally arriving at the doors of the Mother Church of the British Commonwealth.

The Queen was wearing the same rose-pink dress and matching coat and hat that she had worn to the opening of the Olympics in Montreal a year earlier—the outfit wasn't especially memorable, but it struck just the right note of regal matronliness. The Duke of Edinburgh was in the full-dress uniform of an Admiral of the Fleet in his wife's navy. All the nearer members of the royal family were present: Princess Margaret also dressed in pink, recalling 42 years earlier when she and her sister wore the same colors at the service for their grandfather's Jubilee; Princess Anne looking pregnant, which she was; another Duchess of Kent looking stunning. Prince Charles was uniformed in the full-dress rig of Colonel-in-Chief of the Welsh Guards, complete with a high bearskin hat. His bearing was undeniably royal, the result of a lifetime of practice in these kinds of high ceremonies of State.

After the service, the Queen attended a luncheon at the Guildhall given by the Lord Mayor of the City of London. She read a speech reaffirming her coronation vow to pledge her life to the service of her people, and in doing so evidenced a tremendous poise which vast experience on the throne had given her. For the rest of the day and into the

night, she and members of her family made the many oblig-
atory appearances on the palace balcony which great occasions always require. The British people, who were given
the day off as a national holiday, took a consuming pride in
their queen, not just for what she was, but for *who* she was.
She had done damn well these 25 years, and her people
wanted her to know it.

Although not all royal weddings are ceremonies of
State, most have the same elements of pomp and great
pageantry. The Crown understands that a royal wedding
provides a splendid show, generally popularizing the chief
participants as well as the institution of monarchy itself. The
1974 marriage of Princess Anne (not technically a State occasion, which relieved the Princess from the obligation of inviting the entire diplomatic corps and every government
minister) was held at Westminster Abbey, a site purposely
chosen to turn the wedding into an occasion of high pageantry.

One of the features which characterizes British royal
weddings is the display of the bride's gifts, usually in St.
James's Palace. Over 50,000 people paid twenty-five pence
apiece to see Anne's 2,000 presents, which included two Lip-
pizaner horses from Yugoslavia's President Tito.

British schoolchildren were especially excited about the
wedding because it had been declared a national school holiday. The only unpleasant note was struck when the press
found out that *Britannia*, which would take the couple on
their honeymoon, had been newly refitted at a cost of
£2,000,000.

Only a coronation exceeds a royal funeral in majesty
and splendor. The first ceremony following a monarch's
death is the Accession Proclamation of his successor, an act
carried out all over the kingdom in individual assemblages of

great pomp. But the proclamation is only symbolic, in that
the new monarch is fully and instantly monarch on his or
her predecessor's death.

Under most circumstances, the body of a British sovereign or queen consort will lie in state in Westminster Hall
for three days, the coffin on a high catafalque, draped with
the Royal Standard and surmounted by the Imperial State
Crown, Orb and Royal Scepter, surrounded by four Yeoman
Warders, all with bowed heads. For the lying-in-state of
King George VI, 5,000 people each daylight hour for three
days—nearly 300,000 people—filed past this somber but
magnificent scene.

The funeral procession of George VI went through
London from Westminster Hall along Whitehall to the Mall,
up St. James's Street to Piccadilly and Park Lane, finally
ending at Paddington Station, the terminus serving Windsor.
It included dozens of British and foreign royalty, Common-
wealth high commissioners and foreign heads of state; the
American delegate was Secretary of State Dean Acheson.
Immediately following the gun carriage bearing the King's
coffin was the carriage with the Queen, the Queen Mother,
Princess Margaret and the Princess Royal.

After taking the body by train to Windsor, the funeral
service was held in St. George's Chapel, the church so
closely identified with the Order of the Garter and the royal
family itself. The entry into the chapel coincided with the
two-minute silence observed throughout the entire Commonwealth. The funeral concluded when the Lord Chamberlain
broke his staff of office in two and placed the pieces on the
coffin as a symbol that his services to the King were ended.
National mourning continued for three months, as for any
sovereign, while family mourning went on for a year.

For all royal weddings and funerals, except the funeral
of the sovereign, the Comptroller of the Lord Chamberlain's
office is in overall charge of the ceremonial arrangements.

For a monarch's funeral, the Earl Marshal presides, as he does for coronations. And in connection with funerals, it should be noted that British sovereigns never—well, almost never—attend any except those of close relatives. A precedent-breaking exception was Queen Elizabeth II's attendance at the St. Paul's services for Sir Winston Churchill. Her presence at Lord Mountbatten's funeral was unusual in that he was only distantly related to the Queen herself.

One final symbolic token of the monarch's passing is the tolling of Big Ben—once each minute for every year of the sovereign's life. The last time this mournful sound reverberated from the Clock Tower of Westminster Palace was in 1952, lasting for 56 minutes as it paced off the years of King George VI.

8

The Bill
COST ACCOUNTING
BRITAIN'S HERITAGE

Inflation is a plague for almost everyone these days, not the least the Queen of England. Her financial difficulties have become common knowledge to even the smallest of her subjects, one of whom thought the Queen might actually be in want. While she was visiting his nursery school in London, four-year-old Jesse Hill unceremoniously managed to scamper up to the Queen and press a ten-pence coin into her gloved palm. "Here you are, Queen. I want to help you with your palace." Momentarily flustered, she pocketed it, but later returned it to Jesse's teacher. A moving vignette, but none need worry that the royal family is anytime soon going to have to stop living in the manner to which they alone of their countrymen are still accustomed.

The only issue of any real controversy surrounding Britain's royal family today is its cost and the manner in which it is financed. The fairness or unfairness of being ruled—even though the ruling is totally theoretical rather than actual—by a person who inherited the job isn't much agonized over. The principle of hereditary monarchy is so ingrained in the average Briton's psyche that most concern themselves only with the merits of a particular monarch, not the basic justice of the system itself. Antimonarchism doesn't even form a political undercurrent in the United Kingdom. But when the question of paying for the Crown, its wearer and her dependents periodically arises, the issue hottens up considerably—questions in Parliament, letters to the *Times*, rebuttals from the palace Press Secretary. It therefore seems useful to examine the Court's historical income and expenses, and to look at the delicate way in which the modern royal chimera is funded.

Until the beginning of the reign of King George III in 1760, the sovereign personally paid for a great array of the official expenses of running the country, including the salaries of all civil servants, ambassadors and judges, and the enormous upkeep of the palaces and the royal household. In order to keep up with these expenses, a large number of hereditary revenues went to the Crown, including the rights to all treasure trove, mines, fish and swans, all tithes of bishoprics during their vacancies, certain customs duties, taxes on beer, and post-office receipts.

Eventually, even these resources became inadequate, and a new method of providing for the Crown's support had to be found. So the new king, George III, agreed to turn over most of these hereditary earnings, and in their place he would receive an annual grant from Parliament called the Civil List. Out of this amount, first set at £800,000, he still had to pay, in addition to personal expenses, the salaries of the Civil Service and ambassadors, hefty drains on his new pay packet which continued until the beginning of the reign of King William IV in 1830. Most were then removed, and the amount of the grant was reduced to £510,000.

The Civil List (which was until very recent years never changed once it was reviewed and adjusted at the beginning of each new reign) still formed only part of the sovereign's income, being supplemented by monies from Crown Estates, lands most of which had been sequestered from the Church during the time of Henry VIII. George IV traded off most of these mismanaged and almost bankrupt tracts for an additional £50,000 per year. Then and for many years thereafter, the sovereign was getting the best of this deal with Parliament.

The monarch's last item of governmental responsibility, the Secret Service, then costing about £10,000 a year, continued down until Queen Victoria's reign. To rid the Crown totally of all such costs of government, she then made final George IV's bargain with Parliament. The monarch would thereafter retain, in addition to the Civil List, the revenues from only two estates, the duchies of Lancaster and Cornwall, the latter to provide an income for the heir apparent (but never an heir or heiress presumptive). Technically, even today the title for all the former Crown Lands is still vested in the monarch, and one of the first requirements a new monarch confronts on his accession is to sign over the revenues from them (except the two duchies) to the state.

Thus at the beginning of Queen Elizabeth II's reign, she put herself "at the disposal of the House of Commons with regard to the Civil List," according to the bureaucratic formula. A Parliamentary committee meeting with various Household officials recommended an annual Civil List of £475,000 for the remainder of her reign. The amount included a Supplementary Provision of £95,000 a year to keep the allowance ahead of inflation. Out of this sum, the Queen saved enough each year so that when the Civil List became inadequate to meet expenses in the mid-1960s, she was able to dip into reserves for a few more years. The reserves ran out in 1970, and the monarchy went, in the headline-producing words of Prince Philip, "in the red." Negotiations started anew with Parliament, and the results, the Civil List Act of 1972 together with the 1975 Amendment to the Act, are what finances the royal family's official expenses today. At least, *partly* finances them.

Before anything more is said about the Civil List, a very important fact to be borne in mind is that over 75 percent of the expenses incurred in running Britain's monarchy are paid for by departmental appropriations, totally apart from the Civil List. Included are such costly items as *Britannia*, the Queen's Flight, train travel, the upkeep of the palaces (not the Queen's private homes, though), and State visits overseas. The Defense Ministry's tab for *Britannia* in 1977–78 ran to £3,250,000, that for the Queen's Flight at about £1,800,000. The upkeep of the palaces cost the Department of the Environment £4,545,000 in the same period.

These "Department Votes" account for approximately £11,000,000 of the total £14,000,000 annual bill for maintaining Britain's monarchy. Rather a lot, but loyal supporters like to point out that the National Health Service bill for tranquilizers now runs to more than £20,000,000 a year.

Apart from Department Votes, the Queen's expenditures are financed from three sources. First, as we've seen, is the Civil List, the principal funding for Household and other expenses incurred in the course of her duties as Head of State. (The portion going for salaries accounts for about 75 percent of the total List.) As previously mentioned, the Civil List is approved by Parliament, though not always without acrimony. Scottish M. P. Willie Hamilton is famous for his antimonarchist diatribes every time the subject of royal funding comes up in the House of Commons.

The 1972 Act fixed the Civil List at £980,000, a figure which inflation forced Parliament to raise to £1,400,000 by the 1975 Amendment to the Act, which also included a permanent inflation percentage factor. As a result, the Queen's Civil List now stands at £1,950,000, and shows absolutely no sign of going anywhere but up. Ten other members of the royal family each receive their own mini–Civil List, ranging from £175,000 for the Queen Mother and £93,500 for Prince Philip to £59,000 for Princess Margaret and £60,000 for Princess Alexandra of Kent. Prince Charles does not receive a Civil List, the reasons for which will be explained shortly.

The Queen's Civil List is administered by three Royal Trustees—the Prime Minister, the Chancellor of the Exchequer (Britain's equivalent of Secretary of the Treasury), and the Keeper of the Privy Purse, the last a member of the Queen's Household with offices in Buckingham Palace. They are required to review the whole matter of royal finances every 10 years and give their report to Parliament.

Some of the provisions of the Civil List Act are fairly irksome to a large number of Britons. The stipends most often called into question are those for two princesses who seemingly do little to earn their money and begrudge the little they do. Princess Margaret and Princess Anne are both fed very well at the public trough, to the tune of approximately $135,000 per year each. Much of their "work" lies in the rigors of attending occasional film premieres and other such pleasurable activities. This can and does make the eternally penny-pinching Briton question the relevance *not of the Queen*, but certainly of some of her less high-minded relatives.

The Civil List allowances for the royal relatives theoretically represents reimbursement for expenses incurred as part of their royal duties; it is not a salary as such. Oddly, however, the Civil Lists for the Queen's relatives are determined ahead of, not after, the fact. It would seem logical that reimbursement for "costs" would be figured after the costs were incurred, not before. The reasoning that the Civil Lists are reimbursement rather than salary is used to justify the fact that the payments are exempt from income tax.

Even the Queen Mother's allowance of £175,000—over $400,000—is subject to legitimate debate. What indeed can an 80-year-old woman, already immensely comfortable and housed in a string of mansions, possibly do with such an amount? How does the royal family justify a Civil List of £17,262 for the 20-year-old, naval-cadet son of the Queen, regardless of the fact that he is now given only a fraction for "spending money" while the remainder is banked? The Prime Minister's salary is only £10,000 a year more than that of this underage schoolboy. These sorts of questions do tend to give pause to many of the Queen's subjects. Even granted the general esteem in which the monarchy is held, nagging questions about its costs persist.

The Queen's second funding source is the Privy Purse, a designation redolent of Tudor finances. The Privy Purse was originally pretty much what its name implies—the private pocket money of the sovereign. All that has changed. Today the Privy Purse is the money the Queen receives from the duchy of Lancaster (officially the "Duchy and County Palatine of Lancaster") of which she is duke—not duchess, the distinction being a fine old British quirk for its female sovereigns. The duchy was a patchwork of estates built up by various kings in the Middle Ages. The lands (together with those of the duchy of Cornwall—see following) were kept separate from the Crown Estates which were traded off to Parliament in exchange for the Civil List.

Today the duchy is administered by the Chancellor of the Duchy of Lancaster, a political cabinet-level appointment whose primary governmental function is to serve as Minister without Portfolio—meaning a minister without a specifically assigned department, but one whom the Prime Minister can detail to special high-level tasks. Since the beginning of the 1970s, most Chancellors have been assigned to deal with problems of the national economy. Their duties to the actual duchy administration take up a small fraction of their time. The duchy office is in Lancaster Place in the Strand.

Most of the duchy's 52,000 acres are farmland in York-shire, although there are bits all over the country, including London. Since her accession, the Queen has received over £4,000,000 from duchy revenues. They now provide her with about £500,000 each year.

Officially, Privy Purse revenues meet the costs of pri-vate expenditures arising from the Queen's responsibilities as Head of State, such as clothes, robes and uniforms. They also go to form a pension fund for past and present employ-ees not covered by union pensions, and they pay for the maintenance of Sandringham and Balmoral, her non-State-owned homes. The Privy Purse also covers allowances for royal family members who don't have their own Civil Lists. Incidentals such as royal contributions to charity come out of the Privy Purse. Significantly, this source has been used to subsidize Civil List deficits in the past. With the inflation escalation clause now in the Civil List, this should no longer be the case.

The obvious unanswered question about the Lancaster revenues is whether a 20th-century monarch can rightly still "own" vast tracts of land won by medieval forebears, land which well might be thought of as State property rather than Crown property. If the principle of primogeniture is the jus-tification, then any number of distant cousins of the Queen have superior claims to these properties. For example, there was the son of King James II, a prince dumped from the line of succession solely because of his religion. In fact, the duchy "belongs" to the Queen by only the most tenuous logic. Un-fortunately, this sort of peculiarity in the financing of the Crown provides an easy target for critics, and tends to throw shadows on the value and accomplishments of Britain's highly symbolic form of constitutional hereditary monarchy.

The third and final source of the Queen's funding is her own private, and extremely ample, purse. The enormity of Elizabeth II's private fortune is one of the most closely guarded secrets in the world, but there is absolutely no question that her bank accounts, investments, real property, jewels and portfolio are worth many tens of millions of pounds. It is open to considerable uncertainty whether Balmoral and Sandringham (the commercial farming operations of which are highly lucrative) can legitimately be considered the Queen's private property, as opposed to properties inalienable from the person of the sovereign. What is certain is that in 1936 George VI had to buy them from his newly abdicated brother, who had inherited them from his father with the expectation that he would remain King and pass them on in turn to his heir. When Edward VIII chucked it all to marry Mrs. Simpson, he demanded and received a huge sum from his younger brother, money which helped him to live for the rest of his life in the outrageously lavish style to which he had become accustomed.

Certainly, if the generations of monarchs who have inherited these valuable estates had been liable for death duties on them, the properties could not have been bequeathed intact. The same principle can be said to apply to the mountains of jewels the Queen possesses by virtue of her position. (The Crown Jewels, which include the Regalia in the Tower of London, are not the property of the sovereign, but of the State.) The great majority of those in her collection have been handed down from queen to queen. Edward VIII's grandmother, Queen Alexandra, willed jewels worth millions to him, fully expecting his future wife would become queen. His wife didn't become queen, but he gave them to her anyway; she still has them today. When she dies, there are rumors that they will go to the French State by bequest. There are also rumors that if that does happen, the Queen will wage a fierce struggle to get them back where it can be presumed that she expects they belong—in the keeping of the royal family. The present Queen may consider family gems as heirlooms only in her keeping, but Uncle David considered them his strictly for keeps.

The royal collections—everything from stamps and paintings to furniture and books, nearly every conceivable kind of collection, and in the aggregate, priceless—are not the least of the wealth surrounding the Queen. The paintings are spread out all over the royal residences, but those at Windsor are literally among the highest strata of world-class masterpieces. The Queen shows most of them to the public on a kind of rotation basis, even letting all but the da Vinci's and Holbeins be exhibited out of Britain; she feels works by those two artists are simply too much a part of Britain's national artistic treasures to risk any injury from travel. Rooms full of Rembrandts and Van Dycks and Titians, drawers stuffed with da Vinci drawings and Holbein sketches, all go to make up what is the greatest collection of art anywhere outside of a national museum.

All the royal residences have one kind of collection or another. The stamp rooms at Buckingham Palace hold the most complete set of British and Empire stamps in existence, with some individual rarities having values in excess of £1,000,000. At Sandringham, there is Queen Alexandra's Fabergé collection; at Balmoral, the memorabilia of Victoria and Albert, forming just another of the Crown's many unique treasures. At Windsor, there is *everything*—Queen Mary's stunning Doll's House, masses of medieval armor and weapons, a library holding many of the finest and rarest manuscripts ever made (including 100 books printed before 1500, called incunabula, mostly purchased by George IV), tons of gold and silver plate, masses of antique china of museum quality.

None of these collections is considered by the Queen to be at her personal disposal; instead, she calls herself the "nation's guardian" of this embarras de richesses. But the fact remains that she has it to use and enjoy forever, to pass on to her son as part of his inheritance. That pretty much sums up the major attributes of ownership—any encumbrance of title is academic in its effect.

The Queen pays no income tax on *any* of her income, state or private. She is the only person in her kingdom to enjoy such an exemption. All others are liable for taxes on their individual Civil Lists for nonofficial expenses. But since there aren't supposed to be nonofficial expenses paid for by the Civil Lists, the effect is that these family members pay taxes only on private investment income. Even Prince Philip is obligated to pay income tax on private income, but his liability is of course figured without his wife's income counted.

The Queen is exempt from all capital gains taxes or surtaxes (which started to have a meaningful effect in Britain after World War II), including any on her private investments, as well as from transfer taxes and death duties. The latter ensures that the royal estates and collections will be passed on intact to her heir.

This unique tax exemption for the Queen has of course been the primary factor in making the royal family the richest in Britain today. This situation has been a fairly recent development; in the past, many noble land-owning families possessed wealth far in excess of that of the royal family. Its rise to being the wealthiest family in the country has occurred with the greatest rapidity since the forthright income-redistributionist policies of Attlee's postwar Labour government.

Other members of the royal family are vulnerable to death duties. As an example, the Queen Mother's extremely valuable collection of paintings—Manets, Sisleys, and so on—will be liable for valuation for probate unless she gives them over to the Crown.

The moment his mother became Queen, Prince Charles became the 24th Duke of Cornwall, inheriting the revenue from lands wrested by his ancestors many centuries before, in essentially the same way the duchy of Lancaster estates came to the Crown. The duchy of Cornwall is vested in male heirs only; if there is none, it lies dormant in the Crown. Accordingly, Princess Elizabeth could not inherit the duchy revenue, and her father used the income to support his younger brother, the Duke of Gloucester.

The import of the duchy in modern times has rather more to do with its valuable London properties—the Kennington Oval and 45 acres of London's South Bank with 850 tenancies of shops and flats—than with the bleak southern England moors making up most of its 131,000 acres. The duchy is controlled by The Council, a committee of seven members headed by the Marquess of Lothian under the archaic title of Lord Warden of the Stannaries. The offices, staffed with 40 people, are just around the corner from the palace in Buckingham Gate. Unlike the Lancaster chancellorship, The Council has no political influence.

The income from the Cornwall estate now totals about £250,000 per year. By agreement with the government, Prince Charles is not obligated to pay income tax on the revenue, but he agreed in 1969 (when the money first started coming to him) to give up 50 percent to the government, "until such time as he would marry or occur some other change in his circumstances." (His great-uncle David, as Prince of Wales, had set a similar precedent—at the government's insistence—by returning 30 percent of his income to the Treasury.) Thus, in effect, the Prince of Wales's tax bracket is 50 percent, far lower than it would be on the same amount "earned" by anyone else. (Normal taxation would leave him with about £10,000 out of the £250,000; to be left with £125,000, he would have to earn about £5,000,000.) The Prince did turn over his nonprincely naval salary to charity, though.

Prince Charles's actual right to revenues from this source is a legitimate issue of contention. Although it relieves the Civil List of the need to support the monarch's heir, it places his income in an inequitable light, both because he receives money from a source to which no one can still seriously maintain he has an unquestioned moral right, and because he need not pay the same rate of tax that any of his fellow countrymen would be required to pay. As Prince of Wales, Charles works hard and steadily at his job, and certainly deserves recompense just as any other civil servant. But it would take some of the sting out of the monarchy's critics if the legal basis for the Prince's income were moved into the 20th century.

9

Future
KING CHARLES III?

As these closing comments are being written, one of the world's few remaining monarchs has recently given up her throne. At the age of 71, Holland's Queen Juliana feels her "powers are not what they were," and that it was therefore in the best interests of the people of The Netherlands that her eldest daughter, Crown Princess Beatrix, should become their new sovereign.

Although Juliana followed the precedent in which her own mother abdicated in her favor some 30 years earlier, it is somehow sad that a hereditary sovereign should view her job in the same light as that of any of her subjects. As surely as scandal or misdoing, this can only diminish any crown. If this seemingly out-of-date form of governance is to survive, then the central players should stick to the time-honored terms that sovereignty isn't to be put aside as a burden no longer to be comfortably borne.

Hard as it is now to understand the uproar caused by Edward VIII's abdication in the murky past of the mid-thirties, the fact remains that the crisis hit most Britons with the force of a load of bricks. All else may come and go, but the Crown is supposed to be the rock on which the institution of government is based. If it could be discarded so blithely, then where is the sense in continuing it? In this case, it was fortunate for the monarchy as well as for the British people that the injury was so rapidly healed by the character of the new King and his dignified and popular family.

The meaning of modern constitutional monarchy is continuity. What makes this genus of government acceptable for those over whom it holds sway is the rare comfort of knowing one bit of the future with as much certainty as anything beyond the moment can be known. With the hereditary system, people take contentment that the future links them to their past, in their continuum as a united people with a common heritage.

This is the high purpose the British Crown so honorably and competently fulfills today. Even though the country is being torn by social conflict between different classes, the Crown represents *every* Briton, and can accordingly be the symbol which still bonds the people into a nation.

It's not likely that by the time the Prince of Wales ascends the throne these almost insuperable problems will have been solved. King Charles III could well be presented with a kingdom bristling at inherited privilege, of which the monarchy stands out as a prime example. To ensure that the throne lasts long enough to pass on to his heir, Charles will have to convince his people that the Crown will continue to represent the heritage, the traditions and the finest values of Britain.

His surest course for success will be to emulate his mother. It is difficult to find many young people in Britain who nowadays give the monarchy much thought one way or the other; it's fashionable to consider the institution "irrelevant." But when it comes to the Queen herself, it's another story. Elizabeth II has managed to put herself almost beyond criticism, not merely because she wears the crown, but because of the consummately creditable manner in which she has carried out her queenship. It is a trust she determinedly intends to hand over intact to the next king of England. The last great power left to Britain's monarchs is the opportunity to encourage reason and moderation through royal example. With its sovereign today, the country has been fortunate indeed.

The Royal Arms

The Queen's Cipher

Appendices

CHILDREN AND GRANDCHILDREN OF QUEEN VICTORIA AND PRINCE ALBERT

VICTORIA, Empress Frederick of Germany, 1840–1901
   Wilhelm II, Emperor of Germany, 1859–1941
   Charlotte, Duchess of Saxe-Meiningen, 1860–1919
   Henry, 1862–1929
   Sigismund, 1864–1866
   Victoria, Princess of Schaumburg-Lippe, 1866–1929
   Waldemar, 1868–1879
   Sophie, Queen of Greece, 1870–1932
   Margarete, Princess Frederick-Charles of Hesse,
      1872–1954

EDWARD VII, King of England (m. Princess Alexandra of
   Denmark), 1841–1910
   Albert Victor, Duke of Clarence and Avondale,
      1864–1892
   George V, King of England, 1865–1936
   Louise, Duchess of Fife, 1867–1931
   Victoria, 1868–1935
   Maud, Queen of Norway, 1869–1938
   Alexander, 1871 (born April 6, died April 7)

ALICE, Reigning Grand Duchess of Hesse, 1843–1878
    Victoria, Marchioness of Milford Haven, 1863–1950
    Elizabeth, Grand Duchess Sergius of Russia, 1864–1918
    Irene, Princess Henry of Prussia, 1866–1953
    Ernest Louis, Reigning Grand Duke of Hesse,
        1868–1937
    Frederick, 1870–1873
    Alix, Empress (Alexandra) of Russia, 1872–1918
    Mary, 1874–1878

ALFRED, Duke of Edinburgh (m. Grand Duchess Marie of
  Russia), 1844–1900
    Alfred, Prince of Saxe-Coburg, 1874–1899
    Marie, Queen of Rumania, 1875–1938
    Victoria, [1] G. D. Ernest of Hesse, [2] G. D. Cyrill of
        Russia, 1876–1936
    Alexandra, Princess of Hohenlohe-Langenburg,
        1878–1942
    Beatrice, Princess Alfonso of Spain, 1884–1966

HELENA, Princess Christian of Schleswig-Holstein,
  1846–1923
    Christian Victor, 1867–1900
    Albert, Duke of Schleswig-Holstein, 1869–1931
    Helena Victoria, 1870–1948
    Marie Louise, 1872–1956
    Frederick Harold, 1876 (born May 12, died May 20)

LOUISE, Duchess of Argyll, 1848–1939

ARTHUR, Duke of Connaught (m. Princess Louise of Prus-
  sia), 1859–1942
    Margaret, Crown Princess of Sweden, 1882–1920
    Arthur, Duke of Connaught, 1883–1938
    Patricia, Lady Patricia Ramsay, 1886–1972

LEOPOLD, Duke of Albany (m. Princess Helena of
    Waldeck), 1853–1884
        Alice, Countess of Athlone, 1883–1981
        Charles, Duke of Saxe-Coburg-Gotha, 1884–1954

BEATRICE, Princess Henry of Battenberg, 1857–1944
        Alexander, Marquess of Carisbrooke, 1890–1956
        Victoria Eugenia, Queen of Spain, 1887–1969
        Leopold, 1889–1922
        Maurice, 1891–1914

DESCENDANTS
OF KING GEORGE V
AND QUEEN MARY

EDWARD VIII, King of England, later Duke of Windsor (m. Mrs. Wallis Simpson), 1894–1972

GEORGE VI, King of England (m. Lady Elizabeth Bowes-Lyon), 1895–1952
   Elizabeth II, Queen of England (m. Duke of Edinburgh*), 1926–
      Charles, Prince of Wales, 1948–
      Princess Anne, Mrs. Mark Phillips, 1950–
         Peter Phillips, 1977–
      Prince Andrew, 1960–
      Prince Edward, 1964–
   Princess Margaret, Countess of Snowdon, 1930–
      David, Viscount Linley, 1961–
      Lady Sarah Armstrong-Jones, 1964–

*Philip Mountbatten, the former Prince Philip of Greece, was created Duke of Edinburgh the day before his wedding.

MARY, Princess Royal and Countess of Harewood, 1897–1965
  George, Earl of Harewood (m. [1] Marion Stern, [2] Patricia Tuckwell), 1923–
    David, Viscount Lascelles [1], 1950–
    Hon. James Lascelles [1], 1953–
    Hon. Jeremy Lascelles [1], 1955–
    Hon. Mark Lascelles [2], 1964–
  Hon. Gerald Lascelles (m. [1] Angela Dowding [2] Elizabeth Colvin), 1924–
    Henry Lascelles [1], 1953–

HENRY, Duke of Gloucester (m. Lady Alice Montagu-Douglas-Scott), 1900–1974
  Prince William, 1941–1972
  Prince Richard, Duke of Gloucester (m. Birgitte van Deurs), 1944–
    Alexander, Earl of Ulster, 1974–
    Lady Davina Windsor, 1977–
    Lady Rose Windsor, 1980–

GEORGE, Duke of Kent (m. Princess Marina of Greece), 1902–1942
  Prince Edward, Duke of Kent (m. Katharine Worsley), 1935–
    George, Earl of St. Andrews, 1962–
    Lady Helen Windsor, 1964–
    Lord Nicholas Windsor, 1970–
  Princess Alexandra, the Hon. Mrs. Angus Ogilvy, 1936–
    James Ogilvy, 1964–
    Marina Ogilvy, 1966–
  Prince Michael (m. Baroness Marie-Christine von Reibnitz), 1942–
    Lord Frederick Windsor, 1979–

JOHN, 1905–1919

THE ENGLISH TITLED SYSTEM
SIMPLIFIED

RANK & NUMBERS*	STYLE & TITLE	FORMAL STYLE
Royal Duke (4)	His Royal Highness The Duke of . . .	Most High, Most Mighty and Illustrious Prince
Wife	Her Royal Highness The Duchess of . . .	
Sons	If Monarch's Grandson— HRH Prince John of . . . If Monarch's Great GS— Uses Father's 2nd Title	
Unmarried Daughters	If Monarch's Granddaughter— HRH Princess Jane of . . . If Monarch's Great GD— Lady Jane Smith†	
Duke (26)	His Grace The Duke of . . .	Most High, Potent and Noble Prince
Wife	Her Grace The Duchess of . . .	
Sons	Lord John Smith	
Unmarried Daughters	Lady Jane Smith	
Archbishop (2)	The Most Reverend His Grace The Archbishop of	
Marquess (38)	The Most Honorable The Marquess (of) . . .	Most Noble and Potent Prince
Wife	The Most Honorable The Marchioness (of) . . .	
Sons	Lord John Smith	
Unmarried Daughters	Lady Jane Smith	
Earl (222)	The Right Honorable The Earl (of) . . .	
Wife	The Right Honorable The Countess (of) . . .	
Sons	Honorable John Smith	
Unmarried Daughters	Lady Jane Smith	

ADDRESSED AS	ADDRESSED BY SOVEREIGN AS	NOTES
Your Royal Highness		This is not a separate degree of the peerage, but their dignity outranks that of ordinary Dukes.
Your Royal Highness		
If not Royal Highness, Addressed as My Lord or My Lady		If Eldest son is a Prince, he is not known by his Father's second title; if not a Prince he uses the second title as a courtesy title.
Your Grace	Our Right Trusty and Right Entirely Beloved Cousin	Eldest son may use a courtesy title, if available.
Your Grace		"Smith" represents the family name rather than the Father's title name.
My Lord		
My Lady or Madam		
Your Grace		Status as Peer ends if they retire.
My Lord or My Lord Marquess	Our Right Trusty and Entirely Beloved Cousin	Eldest son may use a courtesy title, if available.
My Lady		
My Lord		
My Lady or Madam		
My Lord	Our Right Trusty and Right Well-Beloved Cousin	Eldest son may use a courtesy title, if available.
My Lady		
Sir		
My Lady or Madam		

(Continued)

RANK & NUMBERS*	STYLE & TITLE	FORMAL STYLE
Viscount (144)	The Right Honorable The Viscount . . .	
Wife	The Right Honorable The Viscountess . . .	
Sons	Honorable John Smith	
Unmarried Daughters	Honorable Jane Smith	
Bishop (48)	The Right Reverend The Lord Bishop of . . .	
Baron (550)	The Right Honorable The Lord . . .	
Wife (Baroness)	The Right Honorable The Lady . . .	
Sons	Honorable John Smith	
Unmarried Daughters	Honorable Jane Smith	
Baronet (1,377)	Sir John Smith	
Wife	Lady Smith	
Sons	John Smith, Esquire	
Unmarried Daughters	Jane Smith	
Knight or Dame	Sir John Smith (or Dame Jane Smith)	
Wife	Lady Smith	
Sons	John Smith, Esquire	
Unmarried Daughters	Jane Smith	

ADDRESSED AS	ADDRESSED BY SOVEREIGN AS	NOTES
My Lord My Lady Sir Madam	Our Right Trusty and Well-Beloved Cousin	Eldest sons of Scottish Viscounts and Barons are usually styled "The Master of . . ."
My Lord		Status as Peers ends if they retire.
My Lord My Lady Sir Madam	Right Trusty and Well Beloved	A Baroness in her own right is usually titled "The Rt. Hon. The Baroness . . ." The equivalent of Baron in the Scottish peerage is "Lord of Parliament."
Sir John Lady Smith Sir Madam		
Sir John (Dame Jane) Lady Smith Sir Madam		

*Includes peeresses in their own right, minors, and peers without seats. There are also 330 life barons and baronesses.

†Here and throughout, "Smith" represents the family name rather than the Father's title name.

THE FULL TITLES
OF QUEEN ELIZABETH II

The royal styles and titles in those countries of which the Queen is head of State are as follows:

Australia Elizabeth the Second, by the Grace of God Queen of Australia and Her other Realms and Territories, Head of the Commonwealth.

The Bahamas Elizabeth the Second, by the Grace of God Queen of the Commonwealth of The Bahamas and of Her other Realms and Territories, Head of the Commonwealth.

Barbados Elizabeth the Second, by the Grace of God Queen of Barbados and of Her other Realms and Territories, Head of the Commonwealth.

Canada Elizabeth the Second, by the Grace of God of the United Kingdom, Canada

Canada   and Her other Realms and Territories
(Continued)   Queen, Head of the Commonwealth,
                Defender of the Faith.

Fiji   Elizabeth the Second, by the Grace of
                God Queen of Fiji and of Her other
                Realms and Territories, Head of the
                Commonwealth.

Grenada   Elizabeth the Second, by the Grace of
                God Queen of the United Kingdom of
                Great Britain and Northern Ireland and
                of Grenada and Her other Realms and
                Territories, Head of the Common-
                wealth.

Jamaica   Elizabeth the Second, by the Grace of
                God of Jamaica and of Her other Realms
                and Territories Queen, Head of the
                Commonwealth.

Mauritius   Elizabeth the Second, Queen of Mauri-
                tius and of Her other Realms and Ter-
                ritories, Head of the Commonwealth.

New Zealand   Elizabeth the Second, by the Grace of
                God Queen of New Zealand and Her
                other Realms and Territories, Head of
                the Commonwealth, Defender of the
                Faith.

Papua New Guinea Elizabeth the Second, Queen of Papua
                New Guinea and Her other Realms and
                Territories, Head of the Common-
                wealth.

United Kingdom   Elizabeth the Second, by the Grace of
                         God of the United Kingdom of Great
                         Britain and Northern Ireland and of Her
                         other Realms and Territories Queen,
                         Head of the Commonwealth, Defender
                         of the Faith.

The Republics of Bangladesh, Botswana, Cyprus, Gambia,
Ghana, Guyana, India, Kenya, Malawi, Malta, Nauru, Ni-
geria, Seychelles, Sierra Leone, Singapore, Sri Lanka, Tan-
zania, Trinidad and Tobago, Uganda, and Zambia, together
with the Federation of Malaysia, the Kingdom of Lesotho,
the Kingdom of Swaziland, the Kingdom of Tonga, and the
Independent State of Western Samoa, recognize the Queen
as Head of the Commonwealth.

THE HEREDITARY PEERAGE
(Except Baronies)

The peerages listed are the highest-ranking titles held (except the Duke of Cornwall, whose title of Prince of Wales outranks his dukedom). Many of these peers hold other titles which are of much greater antiquity.

Royal Dukes

Title	Name
Edinburgh	Prince Philip
Cornwall	Charles, Prince of Wales
Gloucester–2nd	Prince Richard
Kent–2nd	Prince Edward

Dukes

Title	Family Name
Abercorn–5th*	Hamilton
Argyll–12th	Campbell
Atholl–10th	Murray
Beaufort–10th	Somerset
Bedford–13th	Russell

*The number after the title represents the present peer's order of succession.

Dukes *(Continued)*

Title	Family Name
Buccleuch & Queensberry–9th & 11th	Montagu-Douglas-Scott
Devonshire–11th	Cavendish
Fife–3rd	Carnegie
Grafton–11th	FitzRoy
Hamilton–15th	Douglas-Hamilton
Leinster–8th	FitzGerald
Manchester–11th	Montagu
Marlborough–11th	Spencer-Churchill
Montrose–7th	Graham
Newcastle–9th	Pelham-Clinton-Hope
Norfolk–17th	Fitzalan-Howard
Northumberland–10th	Percy
Portland–8th	Cavendish-Bentinck
Richmond & Gordon–9th & 4th	Gordon-Lennox
Roxburghe–10th	Innes-Ker
Rutland–10th	Manners
St. Albans–13th	Beauclerk
Somerset–18th	Seymour
Sutherland–6th	Egerton
Wellington–8th	Wellesley
Westminster–6th	Grosvenor

Marquesses

Title	Family Name
Aberdeen & Temair–5th	Gordon
Abergavenny–5th	Larnach-Nevill
Ailesbury–8th	Brudenell-Bruce
Ailsa–7th	Kennedy
Anglesey–7th	Paget
Bath–6th	Thynne
Bristol–6th	Hervey
Bute–6th	Crichton-Stuart
Cambridge–2nd	Cambridge
Camden–5th	Pratt
Cholmondeley–6th	Cholmondeley
Conyngham–7th	Conyngham
Donegall–7th	Chichester
Downshire–7th	Hill
Dufferin & Ava–5th	Hamilton-Temple-Blackwood
Ely–8th	Tottenham

Title	Family Name
Exeter–6th	Cecil
Headfort–6th	Taylour
Hertford–8th	Seymour
Huntly–12th	Gordon
Lansdowne–8th	Petty-Fitzmaurice
Linlithgow–3rd	Hope
Londonderry–9th	Vane-Tempest-Stewart
Lothian–12th	Kerr
Milford Haven–4th	Mountbatten
Normanby–4th	Phipps
Northampton–7th	Compton
Ormonde–7th	Butler
Queensberry–12th	Douglas
Reading–3rd	Isaacs
Salisbury–6th	Gascoyne-Cecil
Sligo–10th	Browne
Townshend–7th	Townshend
Tweeddale–13th	Hay
Waterford–8th	Beresford
Winchester–18th	Paulet
Zetland–3rd	Dundas

Earls

Title	Family Name
Airlie–13th	Ogilvy
Albemarle–10th	Keppel
Alexander of Tunis–2nd	Alexander
Amherst–5th	Amherst
Ancaster–3rd	Heathcote-Drummond-Willoughby
Annesley–9th	Annesley
Antrim–9th	McDonnell
Arran–8th	Gore
Attlee–2nd	Attlee
Avon–2nd	Eden
Aylesford–11th	Finch-Knightley
Baldwin of Bewdley–4th	Baldwin
Balfour–4th	Balfour
Bathurst–8th	Bathurst
Beatty–3rd	Beatty
Belmore–8th	Lowry-Corry
Bessborough–2nd	Ponsonby
Birkenhead–3rd	Smith

Earls *(Continued)*

Title	*Family Name*
Bradford–6th	Bridgeman
Breadalbane & Holland–10th	Campbell
Buchan–16th	Erskine
Buckinghamshire–9th	Hobart-Hampden
Cadogan–7th	Cadogan
Cairns–5th	Cairns
Caithness–20th	Sinclair
Caledon–6th	Alexander
Carlisle–12th	Howard
Carnarvon–6th	Herbert
Carrick–9th	Butler
Castle Stewart–8th	Stuart
Cathcart–6th	Cathcart
Cavan–12th	Lambart
Cawdor–6th	Campbell
Chichester–9th	Pelham
Clancarty–8th	Trench
Clanwilliam–6th	Meade
Clarendon–7th	Villiers
Cork & Orrery–13th	Boyle
Cottenham–8th	Pepys
Courtown–9th	Stopford
Coventry–11th	Coventry
Cowley–7th	Wellesley
Cranbrook–5th	Gathorne-Hardy
Craven–7th	Craven
Crawford & Balcarres–29th & 12th	Lindsay
Cromartie–4th	Mackenzie
Cromer–3rd	Baring
Dalhousie–16th	Ramsay
Darnley–10th	Bligh
Dartmouth–9th	Legge
De La Warr–10th	Sackville
Denbigh & Desmond–11th & 10th	Feilding
Derby–18th	Stanley
Devon–17th	Courtenay
Donoughmore–7th	Hely-Hutchinson
Drogheda–11th	Moore
Ducie–6th	Moreton
Dudley–4th	Ward
Dundee–11th	Scrymgeour-Wedderburn
Dundonald–14th	Cochrane
Dunmore–9th	Murray
Dunraven & Mount Earl–7th	Wyndham-Quin

Title	*Family Name*
Effingham–6th	Howard
Eglinton & Winston–18th & 9th	Montgomerie
Egmont–11th	Perceval
Eldon–5th	Scott
Elgin & Kincardine–11th & 15th	Bruce
Enniskillen–6th	Cole
Erne–6th	Crichton
Erroll–24th	Hay
Essex–9th	Capell
Ferrers–13th	Shirley
Fingall–12th	Plunkett
Fitzwilliam–8th	Wentworth-Fitzwilliam
Fortescue–7th	Fortescue
Gainsborough–5th	Noel
Galloway–13th	Stewart
Glasgow–9th	Boyle
Gosford–7th	Acheson
Gowrie–2nd	Hore-Ruthven
Granard–9th	Forbes
Granville–5th	Leweson-Gower
Grey–6th	Grey
Guilford–9th	North
Haddington–12th	Baillie-Hamilton
Haig–2nd	Haig
Halifax–2nd	Wood
Halsbury–3rd	Giffard
Hardwicke–10th	Yorke
Harewood–7th	Lascelles
Harrington–11th	Stanhope
Harrowby–6th	Ryder
Howe–6th	Curzon
Huntingdon–15th	Hastings
Iddesleigh–4th	Northcote
Ilchester–9th	Fox-Strangways
Inchcape–3rd	Mackay
Iveagh–3rd	Guinness
Jellicoe–2nd	Jellicoe
Jersey–9th	Child-Villiers
Kilmorey–6th	Needham
Kimberley–4th	Wodehouse
Kingston–11th	King-Tenison
Kinnoull–15th	Hay
Kintore–12th	Keith
Kitchener of Khartoum–3rd	Kitchener
Lanesborough–9th	Butler

Earls *(Continued)*

Title	Family Name
Lauderdale–17th	Maitland
Leicester–6th	Coke
Leven & Melville–14th & 13th	Leslie-Melville
Lichfield–5th	Anson
Limerick–6th	Pery
Lindsay–14th	Lindesay-Bethune
Lindsey & Abingdon–14th & 9th	Bertie
Lisburne–8th	Vaughan
Listowel–5th	Hare
Liverpool–5th	Foljambe
Lloyd George of Dwyfor–3rd	Lloyd George
Longford–7th	Pakenham
Lonsdale–7th	Lowther
Lovelace–5th	King
Lucan–7th	Bingham
Lytton–4th	Lytton
Macclesfield–8th	Parker
Malmesbury–6th	Harris
Mansfield & Mansfield–8th	Murray
Mar & Kellie–13th & 15th	Erskine
Mayo–10th	Bourke
Meath–14th	Brabazon
Mexborough–7th	Savile
Midleton–2nd	Brodrick
Minto–6th	Elliot-Murray-Kynynmound
Moray–20th	Stuart
Morley–6th	Parker
Morton–22nd	Douglas
Mount Edgcumbe–7th	Edgcumbe
Munster–6th	FitzClarence
Nelson–8th	Nelson
Newburgh–11th	Rospigliosi
Norbury–6th	Graham-Toler
Normanton–6th	Agar
Northesk–13th	Carnegie
Onslow–7th	Onslow
Oxford & Asquith–2nd	Asquith
Peel–3rd	Peel
Pembroke & Montgomery–17th & 14th	Herbert
Perth–17th	Drummond
Plymouth–3rd	Windsor-Clive
Portarlington–7th	Dawson-Damer

Title	*Family Name*
Portsmouth–9th	Wallop
Powis–6th	Herbert
Radnor–8th	Pleydell-Bouverie
Ranfurly–6th	Knox
Roden–9th	Jocelyn
Romney–7th	Marsham
Roseberry–7th	Primrose
Rosse–7th	Parsons
Rosslyn–7th	St. Clair-Erskine
Rothes–21st	Leslie
Russell–4th	Russell
St. Aldwyn–2nd	Hicks-Beach
St. Germans–9th	Eliot
Scarbrough–12th	Lumley
Seafield–13th	Ogilvie-Grant
Selborne–4th	Palmer
Selkirk–10th	Douglas-Hamilton
Shaftesbury–10th	Ashley-Cooper
Shannon–9th	Boyle
Shrewsbury & Waterford–21st	Chetwynd-Talbot
Snowdon–1st	Armstrong-Jones
Sondes–5th	Milles-Lade
Southesk–11th	Carnegie
Spencer–8th	Spencer
Stair–13th	Dalrymple
Stradbroke–4th	Rous
Strafford–7th	Byng
Strathmore–4th	Bowes-Lyon
Suffolk & Berkshire–21st & 14th	Howard
Swinton–2nd	Cunliffe-Lister
Tankerville–9th	Bennet
Temple of Stowe–7th	Temple-Gore-Langton
Verulam–7th	Grimston
Waldegrave–12th	Waldegrave
Warwick & Brooke–7th	Greville
Wemyss & March–12th & 8th	Charteris
Westmeath–13th	Nugent
Westmorland–15th	Fane
Wharncliffe–4th	Montagu-Stuart-Wortley-Mackenzie
Wicklow–9th	Forward-Howard
Wilton–7th	Egerton
Winchilsea & Nottingham– 16th & 11th	Finch-Hatton
Winterton–7th	Turnour

Earls *(Continued)*

Title	Family Name
Woolton–3rd	Marquis
Yarborough–7th	Pelham
Ypres–3rd	French

Viscounts

Title	Family Name
Addison–3rd	Addison
Alanbrooke–3rd	Brooke
Allenby–2nd	Allenby
Allendale–3rd	Beaumont
Amory–1st	Amory
Arbuthnott–16th	Arbuthnott
Ashbrook–10th	Flower
Astor–4th	Astor
Bangor–7th	Ward
Barrington–11th	Barrington
Bearsted–3rd	Samuel
Blakenham–1st	Hare
Bledisloe–2nd	Bathurst
Bolingbroke & St. John–7th	St. John
Boyd of Merton–1st	Lennox-Boyd
Boyne–10th	Hamilton-Russell
Brentford–3rd	Joynson-Hicks
Bridgeman–2nd	Bridgeman
Bridport–4th	Hood
Brookeborough–2nd	Brooke
Buckmaster–3rd	Buckmaster
Caldecote–2nd	Inskip
Camrose–2nd	Berry
Chandos–2nd	Lyttelton
Chaplin–3rd	Chaplin
Charlemont–13th	Caulfield
Chelmsford–3rd	Thesiger
Chetwynd–2nd	Chetwynd
Chilston–3rd	Akers-Douglas
Churchill–3rd	Spencer
Cobham–11th	Lyttleton
Colville of Culross–4th	Colville
Combermere–5th	Stapleton-Cotton
Cowdray–3rd	Pearson
Craigavon–3rd	Craig

Title	*Family Name*
Cross–3rd	Cross
Daventry–2nd	FitzRoy
Davidson–2nd	Davidson
De L'Isle–1st	Sidney
De Vesci–6th	Vesey
Devonport–3rd	Kearley
Dilhorne–1st	Manningham-Buller
Dillon–20th	Dillon
Doneraile–9th	St. Leger
Downe–11th	Dawnay
Dunrossil–2nd	Morrison
Eccles–1st	Eccles
Esher–4th	Brett
Exmouth–10th	Pellew
Falkland–14th	Cary
Falmouth–9th	Boscawen
Furness–2nd	Furness
Gage–6th	Gage
Galway–11th	Monckton
Gormanston–17th	Preston
Gort–8th	Vereker
Goschen–4th	Goschen
Gough–5th	Gough
Greenwood–2nd	Greenwood
Hall–2nd	Hall
Hambleden–4th	Smith
Hampden–6th	Brand
Hanworth–2nd	Pollock
Harberton–9th	Pomeroy
Hardinge–4th	Hardinge
Hawarden–8th	Maude
Head–1st	Head
Hereford–18th	Devereux
Hill–8th	Clegg-Hill
Hood–6th	Hood
Ingleby–2nd	Peake
Kemsley–2nd	Berry
Knollys–3rd	Knollys
Knutsford–5th	Holland-Hibbert
Lambert–2nd	Lambert
Leathers–2nd	Leathers
Leverhulme–3rd	Lever
Lifford–8th	Hewitt
Long–4th	Long

Viscounts *(Continued)*

Title	Family Name
Mackintosh of Halifax–2nd	Mackintosh
Malvern–3rd	Huggins
Marchwood–3rd	Penny
Margesson–2nd	Margesson
Massereene & Ferrard–13th & 6th	Skeffington
Maugham–2nd	Maugham
Melville–9th	Dundas
Mersey–4th	Bigham
Mills–2nd	Mills
Molesworth–11th	Molesworth
Monck–6th	Monck
Monckton of Brenchley–2nd	Monckton
Monsell–2nd	Eyres-Monsell
Montgomery of Alamein–2nd	Montgomery
Mountgarret–17th	Butler
Muirshiel–1st	Maclay
Norwich–2nd	Cooper
Oxfuird–1st	Makgill
Portman–9th	Portman
Powerscourt–10th	Wingfield
Ridley–4th	Ridley
Rochdale–1st	Kemp
Rothermere–3rd	Harmsworth
Runciman of Doxford–2nd	Runciman
St. Davids–2nd	Philipps
St. Vincent–7th	Jervis
Samuel–3rd	Samuel
Scarsdale–3rd	Curzon
Selby–4th	Gully
Sidmouth–7th	Addington
Simon–2nd	Simon
Slim–2nd	Slim
Soulbury–2nd	Ramsbotham
Southwell–7th	Southwell
Stuart of Findhorn–2nd	Stuart
Templetown–5th	Upton
Tenby–2nd	George
Thurso–2nd	Sinclair
Torrington–11th	Byng
Trenchard–2nd	Trenchard
Ullswater–2nd	Lowther
Valentia–14th	Annesley
Ward of Witley–1st	Ward

Title	*Family Name*
Watkinson–1st	Watkinson
Waverley–2nd	Anderson
Weir–3rd	Weir
Wimborne–3rd	Guest
Younger of Leckie–3rd	Younger

HEREDITARY PEERESSES
IN THEIR OWN RIGHT
(Except Baronesses)

Countesses

Title	*Family Name*
Dysart	Greaves
Loudoun	Abney-Hastings
Mar	Mar
Mountbatten of Burma	Knatchbull
Sutherland	Sutherland

BUCKINGHAM PALACE

Schematic drawings of the three main floors of Buckingham Palace, showing the general plan of the palace's main rooms.

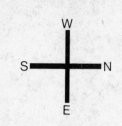

GROUND FLOOR

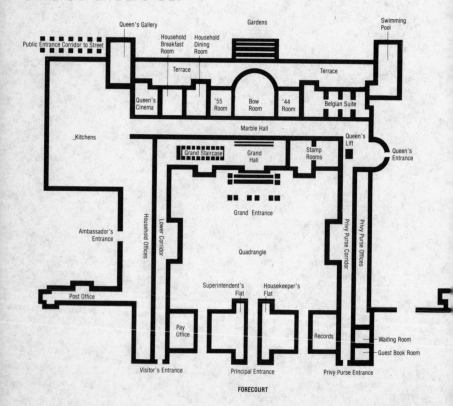

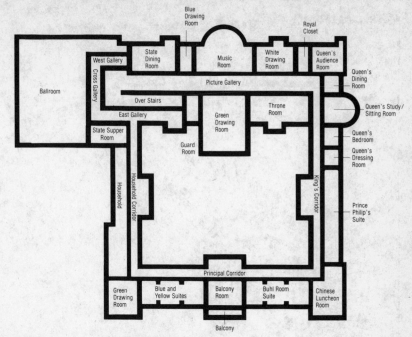

PRINCIPAL FLOOR

Blue Drawing Room

Royal Closet

West Gallery

State Dining Room

Music Room

White Drawing Room

Queen's Audience Room

Cross Gallery

Picture Gallery

Queen's Dining Room

Ballroom

Over Stairs

East Gallery

Green Drawing Room

Throne Room

Queen's Study / Sitting Room

State Supper Room

Queen's Bedroom

Guard Room

Queen's Dressing Room

Household

Household Corridor

King's Corridor

Prince Philip's Suite

Principal Corridor

Green Drawing Room

Blue and Yellow Suites

Balcony Room

Buhl Room Suite

Chinese Luncheon Room

Balcony

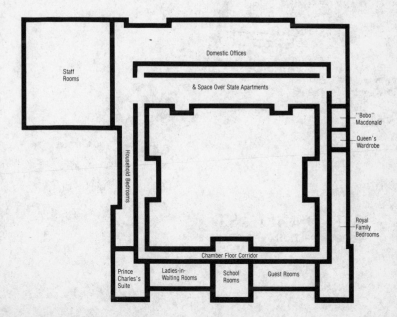

BEDROOM FLOOR

Staff Rooms

Domestic Offices

& Space Over State Apartments

"Bobo" Macdonald

Queen's Wardrobe

Household Bedrooms

Royal Family Bedrooms

Chamber Floor Corridor

Prince Charles's Suite

Ladies-in-Waiting Rooms

School Rooms

Guest Rooms

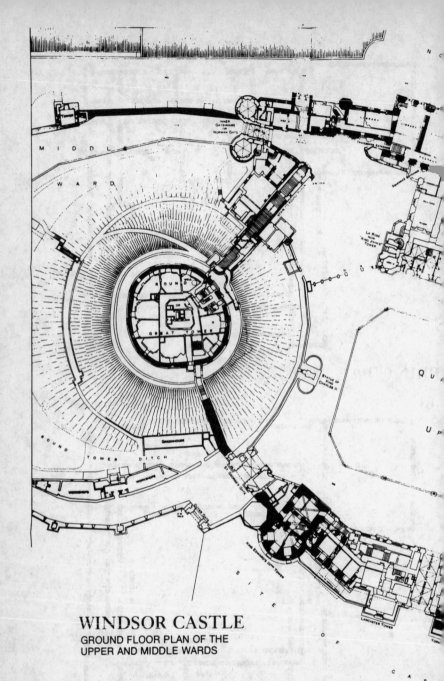

WINDSOR CASTLE
GROUND FLOOR PLAN OF THE
UPPER AND MIDDLE WARDS

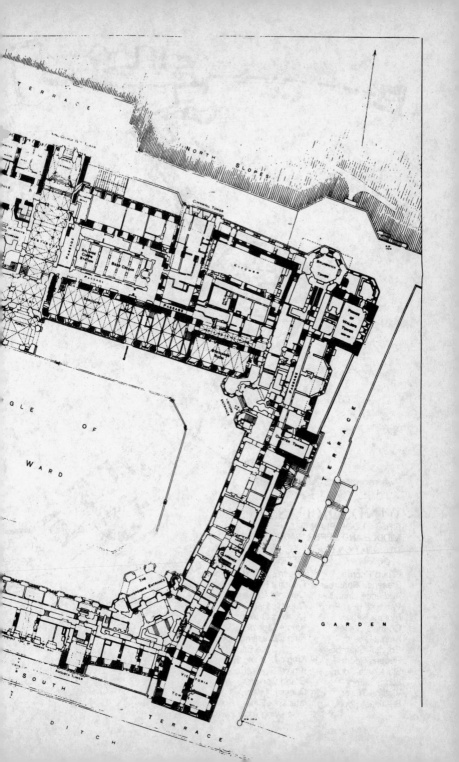

WINDSOR CASTLE
FIRST FLOOR PLAN OF THE MIDDLE AND UPPER WARDS

DESIGNATION ON FLOOR PLAN	DESIGNATION TODAY
Guard Room	Queen's Guard Room
Presence Chamber	Queen's Presence Chamber
Audience Chamber	Queen's Audience Chamber
Vandyke (sic) Room	Queen's Ball Room
Picture Gallery	Queen's Drawing Room
Queen's Closet	King's Closet
King's Closet	King's Dressing Room
Council Chamber	King's State Bedchamber
Rubens Room	King's Drawing Room
State Ante-Room	King's Dining Room
Long Gallery	Grand Corridor
Victoria Tower	Queen's Tower
Breakfast Room	later Oak Dining Room, now used as a living room by the royal family

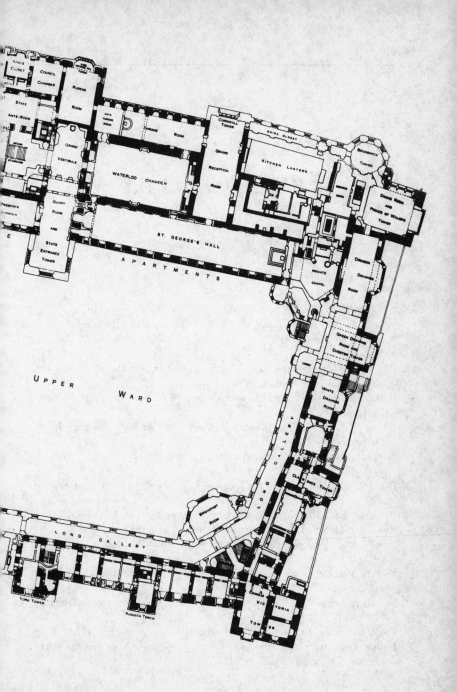

BIBLIOGRAPHY

Albert, Harold A. *The Queen and the Arts*. London: W. H. Allen, 1963.

Annuaire de France. *Royalty, Peerage, and Aristocracy of the World*. Paris: La Nobiliare, 1967.

Aronson, Theo. *Grandmama of Europe—The Crowned Descendents of Queen Victoria*. London: Cassell, 1974.

Barker, Brian. *When the Queen Was Crowned*. London: Routledge & Kegan Paul, 1976.

Benemy, F. W. G. *The Queen Reigns, She Does Not Rule*. London: G. G. Harrop, 1963.

Berkswell Publishing Company. *The Royal Year*, vols. 2, 3, 4, 5. London: 1975–78.

Boothroyd, J. Basil. *Philip: An Informal Biography*. New York: McCall Publishing, 1971.

Braddon, Russell. *All the Queen's Men*. London: Hamish Hamilton, 1977.

Brandeth, Gyles. *A Royal Scrapbook*. London: Michael Joseph, 1972.

Brook-Little, John. *The British Monarchy in Colour*. Poole: Blandford Press, 1976.

Brown, Michele. *Queen Elizabeth II—The Silver Jubilee Book*. London: David & Charles, 1976.

Bryan, Joseph & Charles Murphy. *The Windsor Story*. New York: Morrow, 1979.

Burke's Peerage, Ltd. *Guide to the British Monarchy*. London: 1977.

Butler, Colonel Sir Thomas. *The Crown Jewels and the Coronation Ritual*. London: Pitkin Pictorials, 1976.

Coats, Peter. *The Gardens of Buckingham Palace*. London: Michael Joseph, 1978.

Country Life. Coronation Issue for Queen Elizabeth II. London: 1953.

Daily Express. Queen Mary, A Picture Pageant. London: 1950.

———. *Coronation Souvenir Book*. London: 1937.

Davis, William, ed. *Punch and the Monarchy*. London: Hutchinson, 1977.

Debrett's Peerage, various editions. London: Odhams Press.

———. *Dictionary of the Coronation*. London: Dean & Son, Ltd., 1902.

De La Bere, Brig. General Sir Ivan. *Queen's Orders of Chivalry*. London: Spring Books, 1964.

Desautels, Paul E. *The Gem Kingdom*. New York: Ridge Press, 1970.

Diesbach, Ghislain de. *Secrets of the Gotha*. London: Chapman & Hall, Ltd., 1964.

Duncan, Andrew. *The Queen's Year—The Reality of Monarchy*. New York: Doubleday, Garden City, 1970.

Edgar, Donald. *Happy & Glorious*. London: Barker, 1977.

———. *The Queen's Children*. London: Barker, 1978.

Edwards, Anne. *The Queen's Clothes*. London: Express Books, 1977.

Ehrenskrood, Hans F. von. *Fuerstlicher Haeuser, Genealogisches Handbuch des Adels*. Gluecksberg: C. A. Starke, 1951–53.

Ellis, Hamilton. *The Royal Trains*. London: Routledge, 1975.

Fawcett, Frank. *Court Ceremonial*. Aldershot: Gale & Polden, 1937.

Fletcher, Ifan K. *The British Court—Its Traditions and Ceremonials*. London: Cassell & Co., 1953.

Frost, Conrad. *Coronation, June 2, 1953*. London: Barker, 1978.

Goring, O. G. *From Goring House to Buckingham Palace*. London: Ivor Nicholson & Watson, 1937.

Graeme, Bruce. *A Century of Buckingham Palace*. London: Hutchinson & Co., 1937.

Graves, Charles. *Palace Extraordinary—The Story of St. James's*. London: Cassell, 1963.

Hall, Angus. *Charles—An Illustrated Souvenir*. London: Phoebus, 1977.

Hall, Zillah. *Coronation Costume*. London: Her Majesty's Stationery Office, 1973.

Hamilton, Willie. *My Queen and I*. London: Quartet Books, 1975.

Harris, John, G. de Bellaigue, and Millar, O. *Buckingham Palace and Its Treasures*. New York: Viking, 1968.

Harris, Leonard. *Long to Reign Over Us?* London: Kimber, 1966.

Hedley, Olwen. *Queen's Silver Jubilee*. London: Pitkin, 1977.

Hepworth, Philip. *Royal Sandringham*. Norwich: Wensum Books, 1978.

Heywood, Valentine. *British Titles*. London: A & C Black, 1951.

Hibbert, Christopher. *The Court of St. James's*. London: Weidenfeld & Nicolson, 1979.

Holden, Anthony. *Charles, Prince of Wales*. London: Weidenfeld & Nicolson, 1979.

Howard, Philip. *The British Monarchy in the 20th Century*. London: Hamish Hamilton, 1977.

Hussey, Christopher. *Clarence House*. London: Country Life, Ltd., 1949.

IPC Magazines, Ltd. *Jubilee—A Celebration of the Queen's Silver Jubilee*. London: 1977.

James, G. P. L. *The Royal Family Order* (1951) and Supplement (1954). Washington, D.C.: Collection of the Library of Congress.

Lacy, Robert. *Majesty*. New York: Harcourt Brace Jovanovich, 1977.

Lemoine, Serge. *The Royal Family At Home and Abroad*. Cheltenham: This England, 1977.

————. *A Complete Pictorial Record of the Silver Jubilee Year*. New Malden: Colour Library International, 1977.

Lindsay, Sir Martin of Dowhill, Bart. *The Baronetage*. Privately published by M. Lindsay, Old Vicarage, Woking, Surrey, 1977.

Liversidge, Douglas. *Queen Elizabeth II*. London: Barker, 1974.

————. *Prince Philip*. London: Barker, 1976.

————. *The Queen Mother*. London: Barker, 1977.

London Illustrated News. London: various commemorative issues.

Longford, Elizabeth. *The Royal House of Windsor*. New York: Knopf, 1974.

Mackenzie, Compton. *The Queen's House—A History of Buckingham Palace*. London: Hutchinson, 1953.

Mackworth-Young, Sir Robin. *Windsor Castle*. London: Pitkin Pictorials, 1977.

Martin, Kingsley. *Magic of the British Monarchy*. Boston: Little, Brown, 1962.

McGowan, A. P. *Royal Yachts*. London: Her Majesty's Stationery Office, 1977.

Michie, Alan A. *God Save the Queen*. New York: William Sloane Associates, 1952.

Miller, H. Tatlock. *Royal Album*. London: Hutchinson, 1951.

Montagu of Beaulieu, Lord. *More Equal Than Others*. London: St. Martin's Press, 1970.

Morshead, Sir Owen. *Windsor Castle*. London: Phaidon Press, 1957.

Mosley, Leonard and Robert Haswell. *The Royals*. London: Leslie Frewin, 1966.

Peacocke, Marguerite. *The Story of Buckingham Palace*. London: Odhams Press, 1951.

Penguin Books. *The Queen*. Harmondsworth: 1977.

Pinches, J. H. and R. V. *The Royal Heraldry of England*. Rutland, Vermont: Charles Tuttle, 1974.

Pine, L. G. *The Story of Titles*. Rutland, Vermont: Charles Tuttle, 1969.

Plumb, J. H. and Huw Wheldon. *The Treasures of the British Crown*. New York: Harcourt Brace Jovanovich, 1977.

Pope-Hennessy, James. *Queen Mary*. New York: Knopf, 1960.

Regan, Simon. *Charles, The Clown Prince*. London: Everest Books, 1977.

Spencer-Shew, Betty. *Pomp and Circumstance*. London: Macdonald, 1950.

Sutherland, Donald and Anthony Purdy. *The Royal Homes and Gardens—A Private View*. London: Leslie Frewin, 1966.

Talbott, Godfrey. *Country Life Book of Queen Elizabeth The Queen Mother*. New York: Crescent Books, 1978.

Thompson, J. A. and Arthur Mejia, Jr. *The Modern British Monarchy*. New York: St. Martin's Press, 1971.

Twining, Lord. *A History of the Crown Jewels of Europe*. London: Batsford, 1960.

Vickers, Hugo. *We Want the Queen*. London: Debrett's Peerage, Ltd., 1977.

Whitaker's Almanack. London: various editions.

White, Ralph, and Fisher, Graham. *The Royal Family*. New York: David McKay, 1969.

Williams, Neville, *Royal Residences of Great Britain—A Social History*. New York: Macmillan, 1960.

Young, Shiela. *The Queen's Jewellery*. London: Ebury Press, 1968.

Ziegler, Philip. *Crown and People*. London: Collins, 1978.

Index

NOTE: Where a page number(s) is in **boldface,** it represents the primary reference or description. Royalty and nobility with the same name or title are listed in historical sequence.

227